The Healing of
Rodolphe Grivel

FABRE D'OLIVET (1768–1825)

THE HEALING OF RODOLPHE GRIVEL

CONGENITAL DEAF-MUTE

A Series of Letters written

By

Fabre d'Olivet

Done into English by

Nayán Louise Redfield

Hermetica

San Rafael, Ca

Second, facsimile edition
Hermetica, 2007
First edition, G.P. Putnam's Sons, 1927

For information, address:
Hermetica, P.O. Box 151011
San Rafael, California 94915, USA

Library of Congress Cataloging-in-Publication Data

Fabre d'Olivet, Antoine, 1767–1825
The healing of Rodolphe Grivel: congenital deaf-mute
/Fabre D'Olivet; translated by Nayán Redfield. — Reprint ed.

p. cm.
"First Edition, G.P. Putnam's Sons, NY, 1927."
Includes bibliographical references.
ISBN-13: 978-1-59731-203-5 (pbk.: alk. paper)
ISBN-13: 978-1-59731-228-8 (hardcover: alk. paper)
1. Grivel, Rodolphe, b. 1796. 2. Deaf—Biography.
I. Redfield, Nayán Louise. II. Title.
RF320.F33 2007
362.197'80092—dc22   2007027047
[B]

To

THOSE WHO HAVE REMOVED

THE SANDALS OF TIME

FROM

THE FEET OF LIFE

AND HAVE ENTERED INTO

THE SECRET PLACE;

WHO FROM

THE GREEN GOBLET OF WISDOM

HAVE DRUNK AT

THE FOUNTAIN OF CAUSE

THIS VOLUME

IN FAITH

IS DEDICATED

TO THE READER

THE first edition of this work appeared in 1811, under the title of *Guérison de Rodolphe Grivel, sourd-muet de naissance,* with secondary title, *Notions sur le Sens de l'Ouïe.* In the second edition, 1819, the title stands as *Notions sur le Sens de l'Ouïe, en général, et en particulier sur le Développement de ce Sens opéré chez Rodolphe Grivel et chez plusieurs autres enfants sourds-muets de naissance.* In this volume the Translator has included with the text of the two editions various associative data which she has found in the Bibliothèque Nationale, in the Bibliothèque de la Société de l'Histoire du Protestantisme français, and from private sources.

N. L. R.

TRANSLATOR'S FOREWORD

ANTOINE FABRE D'OLIVET, as savant, philosopher and scholar, needs no introduction to the readers of this book. His *Hermeneutic Interpretation of the Origin of the Social State of Man, Golden Verses of Pythagoras, Hebraic Tongue Restored,* and *Cain,* are already known to the English literary world. In the present work he is shown as humanitarian, revealing himself in this light through circumstances of more than passing interest.

His twelve years of scientific seclusion were devoted to study, which, according to his own words, became his occupation and his relaxation. One of the causes of this forced seclusion would seem to be the result of his literary connection with certain journals in which his articles attracted the jealous attention of Bonaparte and aroused his anger. He was associated with *La Palladium de la Constitution,* a political and literary journal which bore as epigraph: "Vouloir changer sans cesse

de gouvernement, c'est s'exposer à changer sans cesse de vêtements ensanglantés."* This journal, which began August 18th, 1797, was suppressed September 5th of the same year and replaced May 20th, 1798, by *L'Invisible*, a political, literary and moral paper with the epigraph:
"Infert se saeptus nebula, mirabile dictu!
  Per medios, miscetque viris; neque cernitur ulli."**
This publication was interrupted September 3rd, 1798, and reappeared October 2nd, 1798, under the title of *L'Avant Coureur*, a political and literary journal, with "Vives acquirit eundo"† as epigraph.

It was upon Bonaparte's accession to the Consulate, December 24th, 1799, that he began to persecute Fabre d'Olivet because of his ideas, and it is probable that Bonaparte's anger was aroused at this time by some articles appearing in the *Journal des Hommes libres* and signed with the

---

* "To wish for a continual change of government is to expose oneself to a continual change of blood-stained garments."
** "Veiled in a cloud he enters, wondrous to relate,
Through their midst, and mingles with the people, seen by none!"
                                                Æneid, Bk. I, 1.440.
† "One acquires strength in progress."
                                                Æneid, Bk. IV, 1.175.

initial F; for not long after Fabre d'Olivet was included in a decree of proscription banishing two hundred persons to the desert coasts of Africa. However, through the influence of Comte Lenoir de la Roche, then senator, his name was stricken from the list of deportations in 1801.

But in order to preserve his liberty, this peaceful man of letters, who had passed through the Revolution respected equally by the opposed parties, was forced to live in strictest retirement for twelve years. During these years of study, whenever he had finished a book and it was ready to be published [*Le Troubadour* (1803), the first edition of *Notions sur le Sens de l'Ouïe* (1811), *Les Vers Dorés de Pythagore* (1813) etc.], he inserted among its pages various complimentary phrases and praises, by way of cajoling Napoleon's bad temper, so that the book might be printed.

Fabre d'Olivet was not the only writer who was a victim of Napoleon's small mindedness regarding new or liberal ideas. Madame de Staël, it is known, was exiled not only on account of advanced opinions, but also because she would not mention him in her books. History relates that during her exile she was often informed by agents of the government that she might easily put an end to the inconveniences she suffered by publishing a few pages in praise of the Emperor. Bonaparte, in alluding to her talents said, "Madame de Staël carries a quiver full of arrows that would hit a man if he were seated on a rainbow!" Nothing, however, could force from her a single line of flattery.

Toward the end of 1810, Fabre d'Olivet, having completed his *La Langue Hébraïque Restituée*, was introduced by a friend to M. de Montalivet, Minister of the Interior, through whose influence he hoped the book might be published. He was received with much distinction by the Minister who, profoundly impressed by the immensity of the work, appeared disposed to have it printed at the expense of the government. Nevertheless, at their next meeting, the Minister limited his offer to the printing of one volume, that is, the grammar and the radical vocabulary, holding back the translation of the Cosmogony of Moses. Fabre d'Olivet refused this offer abruptly and a rather lively discussion ensued, during which, he says, "sprung the first thought which led me to develop the sense of hearing in a congenital deaf-mute."

Monsieur de Montalivet said that if the Cosmogony of Moses contained all the secrets of the Egyptian priesthood and developed in a few pages the principles of all the sciences, then Fabre d'Olivet should know them, and he concluded, "Demonstrate for me a single one of these principles, and I will have the whole of your work printed."

It was then that Fabre d'Olivet, somewhat nettled as he himself admits, sought out young Rodolphe Grivel, a congenital deaf-mute, pupil in the institution of M. l'abbé Sicard, and being educated there at the expense of the French government. He healed him. The present volume is the history of this healing, together with the jealousies, calumnies and persecutions which followed this amazing deed.

Nayán Louise Redfield.

Hartford, Conn.,
January, 1927.

CONTENTS

APPENDIX

The Healing of Rodolphe Grivel

PRELIMINARY NOTICE

(1st EDITION, 1811)

PRELIMINARY NOTICE

(1st Edition, 1811)

A LETTER written by a student of theology, named Lombard, to the editors of the *Gazette de France*, and published in that paper on March 3rd, 1811, announced my good fortune in procuring the power of hearing and speech for young Rodolphe Grivel, congenital deaf-mute, pupil at that time in the *Institution des Sourds-Muets* under the direction of Monsieur Sicard.*

In a century less enlightened and under a government less protective of the sciences, such a publication would undoubtedly have alarmed me. If I had felt cause for fear, however, I should not have exposed myself; I should have known, even as those ancients who have given me precept and example, how to study nature in silence and carefully to guard her secrets. The saying of Fontenelle would have come to my mind; and

---

* A copy of this letter in full appears on page 231. *Translator.*

instead only of shutting my hand, as he counsels,
I should also have hid it in my mantle.   But in
a time of darkness the light befriends with its
rays.   One is no longer magician, heretic, or sor-
cerer in an Empire where the Monarch, sowing his
course with prodigies and extolling only the one
God, the people are no longer given over to foreign
superstitions.   Where the torches of fanaticism
are extinguished, those of truth are always lighted.
In order to do good one can try the forces of nature,
and leave the common highway without fearing
the dull darts that ignorance itself denies.   Calumny can, it is true, still pursue the one who
dares to thrust back the limits of the human
mind; for men in general, and above all those
who believe themselves savants, object to being
told that they are not at the summit of knowledge.   Idle frivolity and envious indolence can
also fling certain sarcasms and feign to laugh with
ridiculing grins.   But what man is so weak in
courage, who, having devoted himself to the service of humanity, would recoil before such enemies?   If he scorn fortune, if he know how to
appreciate glory, if his life appear to him only
what it really is,—a transient storehouse, the good

usage of which constitutes the reward,—is he not shielded from their attacks? Strong of conscience and proud of the future, does he not know that the triumph of truth, although retarded, is none the less irresistible?

Urged by disinterested motives and wishing to offer to the savant world a rare phenomenon, which I believe adapted to solve one of the most difficult problems of philosophy, that of the origin of speech and the formation of ideas, I have turned to account certain knowledge, drawn from the traditions of the Orient. Attempting a bold experiment, which Providence has deigned to assist, I have opened the ears of a youth congenitally deaf, and I have even enabled him to talk with his fellowmen, enjoying as they do the advantages of speech. This experiment has been attacked as it must necessarily have been. One has tried to corrupt its motives; one has wished to throw doubt upon its success; one has spread the most disparaging and the most injurious rumours. Had I sought only a frivolous glory, or only a base interest, I might skillfully have profited by this disturbance to make an advantageous fame and attract to myself the crowd of credulous patients

who are always ready to give themselves over to
the first presumptuous individual who offers to
heal them. But I have acted, whatever may be
said, from the noblest sentiments by which one
can be animated.

When I determined to have the following letters to my friend printed, it was less to reply to
certain ephemeral diatribes than to give an account to the public of the motives of my conduct,
placing before them the results of my experiment,
and making it possible for true philosophers and
thinking men to obtain therefrom the fruits I
promised to give them. I trust that if their
attention is not too inadvertent, and if they will-
ingly accord me a confidence exempt from prejudices, they will be able, beside the preliminary
data necessary to the solution of the metaphysical
problem of which I have spoken, to find therein
ideas sufficiently elaborated upon the physical
constitution of the sense of hearing, to conceive
as I have, the causes which are opposed to its
development, and perhaps to discover their remedy.

But as the utility of an experiment depends
greatly upon its authenticity, I am about to state
the facts that establish this one by making known

the young man who was its subject. I shall reply afterward in a few words to the principal objections that have been raised.

Rodolphe Grivel was born at Aubonne in Switzerland, May 15th, 1796, of a father and mother of sound constitution, but who soon had the sorrow of perceiving that their son was menaced with absolute deafness. The unfruitful care given him by the two physicians of Aubonne, MM. Gay and Prelaz, from the first months after his birth, confirmed them in their fears. They were left without hope when they saw this child arrive at the age of two or three years without giving a sign of audition or uttering any of the words appropriate to his age. They did not lose courage, however; and neglecting nothing that a comfortable fortune made possible, they consulted one after another the most celebrated physicians of Lausanne and Geneva. Successively MM. Jurine, Maunoir and Butini saw young Grivel and treated him for a long time. Upon him and upon the organ, the use of which he was deprived, they tried all the resources of their art. Electricity and galvanism were used, he bore setons and cauteries, and vesicatories were applied to him; he was

given internally and externally all possible remedies. Nothing worked; he remained completely
deaf, and could understand only by the signs
that nature and need indicated to him. The only
words he pronounced at the age of nine years were
those common to all mutes, results of the joint
action of the labial consonants, *mama, papa, bobo,*
etc.

At this time, his parents having renounced the
hope of seeing him ever enjoy the sense of hearing,
resolved to procure for him at least the advantages
attached to a good education. They decided to
place him, at their own expense, in the *Institution
des Sourds-Muets* at Paris, under the direction of
M. Sicard. During the six years that he remained
in this institution, and while he received the lessons
that were given to children deprived, as he was, of
hearing and speech, he often appeared, and with
approbation, at the public meetings in which
M. Sicard presented him justly as one of the
pupils most distinguished for intelligence. It is
known well enough how they arrived at making
him pronounce certain syllables by mechanical
means, sometimes pinching his arms, sometimes
pressing his throat with the thumb.

It appears that, in the early days of his sojourn
at the *Institution des Sourds-Muets,* he was attacked by a malady which necessitated the care
of M. Itard. This physician, judging favourably
of Rodolphe's intellectual faculties, wrote to his
mother offering to treat him for his deafness; and
in case his cure should be impossible, at least to
demonstrate visibly in him the mechanism of
speech, by making him articulate by imitation.
He did not doubt, he said, that by exercise his
memory would succeed in retaining this mechanism, although he might not be able to show its
results. But M. Itard's proposition meant an
increase of expenses, and the purchase of certain
costly acoustic instruments, and Madame Grivel,
now a widow, had experienced a reverse of fortune. She therefore found herself not only unable to profit by the offer of M. Itard, but obliged
shortly to withdraw her son from the institution,
being unable any longer to continue to pay even
his simple tuition.

She notified the authorities of this unhappy
condition, and asked them to send her son back
to her; but fortunately for young Grivel, his good
conduct and his application had made protectors

for him in all his teachers.   Upon the report presented in favour of this youth, the authorities resolved to keep him, by allowing him, although of Swiss nationality and consequently considered a foreigner, to enjoy the benefits of His Majesty, the Emperor and King.   He was kept as pupil of the *Institution des Sourds-Muets* at the expense of the French government, reckoning from the month of September, 1807.

In the meantime his mother, all of whose tenderness was centred upon the boy after the loss of her husband, the death of her other children, and the vanishing of her fortune, accepted a place as *sous-maîtresse* in the boarding-school of Madame Servier, instructress of young ladies in Paris. Thus she was nearer to this only remaining child who was her sole consolation. It was in this boarding-school, with which my wife was associated, that several times I had the occasion of seeing young Rodolphe when on a visit to his mother. I was touched by the affection he showed her and felt that his natural tendencies might make a commendable man of him if they were not dulled by his infirmity. In order to enable him to enjoy the sense of hearing, and to

make it possible for him to enlighten us upon
many important points of metaphysics, I resolved
to attempt a difficult means, unknown by the
modern savants and physicians, but very well
known by the ancients.   My meditations upon the
traditions of the Chinese, Parsees, Brahmans and
Egyptians, the long and recent study I had made
of the writings of Moses and chiefly of the Cosmogony of that hierographic writer all proved
to me that this means, taught and practised in the
ancient sanctuaries, was not illusory; and that it
must still succeed if Providence deigned to approve of its employment.   I proposed this means
to Madame Grivel, who consented to try it.
Under pretext of the New Year vacation she withdrew her son for several days from the *Institution
des Sourds-Muets*, and placed him with me.   The
7th of January, the first proof of my remedy was
made in her presence, when Providence, invoked,
assisted my efforts.   The obstacle which, from the
birth of this child, had deprived him of the sense
of hearing, yielded, as will be shown further on in
the letters that I am publishing.

Such is the simple and truthful statement of
the facts.   I pray the reader to give a moment's

attention, for it is from these very facts that I am about to draw all my answers to the objections that have been raised.

It has been said, from the first instant when the rumour was spread that a congenital deaf-mute had been healed by my efforts, that this healing was not true, because it was impossible, and that it must necessarily be that the marks of audition given by the deaf-mute were the result of a clever charlatanism.

First I remark that there is nothing impossible in nature except that which involves contradiction. Now, what does one see of contradiction in the cure I have made? I have developed in the auditive organ the auditive faculty, and nothing more. It is true that some very able doctors do not know how, but that is not my fault. Why do they restrict all that is possible to the sphere of their attainments? Must nature be slave to their conventions? Let them dare to interrogate her in her sanctuary! They will then see that the limits of her empire are not placed precisely where they think. As to the charlatanism which they bestow upon me without knowing me, I advise them to come quickly and study its source;

for if they wait too long, Rodolphe himself will be well able to show them the results, by replying aloud to their learned questions.

But if, even in its principle, the cure is confirmed by able men of wisdom and of probity; if, moreover, time assures its evidence, will there remain a refuge for incredulity? Yes, undoubtedly, incredulity will say that the deaf-mute who hears and who speaks has always heard and spoken.

What a miserable objection! In order to have any force, it would have to be shown that the deafness was accidental, occurring at an age when the child was capable of feigning it, or at least that the one who was supposed to be healed was an obscure child, whose origin might present doubts. But it seems that in this case Providence willed beforehand to accumulate the witnesses. All Paris knew Rodolphe Grivel; and knew him as deaf-mute. He was seen a hundred times at the public entertainments of M. Sicard, with whom he passed six years, of which more than three were at the expense of the government. The physician for the deaf-mutes, M. Itard, treated him in his illnesses; he made an offer to his mother to try to heal him of his deafness, and in case he did not succeed at the end of a year, to demonstrate to her the mechanism of speech by making the youth articulate by imitation and without hearing. At the age of nine, when this child entered the institution, he left the hands of the most skillful physicians of Geneva. When younger he had been seen by those of Lausanne; when still younger, by those of Aubonne, the place of his birth. Supposing that from his mother's breast, he had formed the bizarre plan of deceiving all the men who should assemble to observe him, one could not find the moment when such an unheard-of artifice began,—an artifice much more strange, assuredly, than the healing he would have counterfeited.

This appears unanswerable. "Not at all," declares skepticism, "for nature alone can have healed him."

Yes, in the space of two or three thousand years, there have been two or three examples of a similar phenomenon. Then instead of a remedy, I ought to have used a certain divinatory art, to let it be known at the proper moment that among the multitude of deaf-mutes which the French Empire contains, there was one who, congenital

deaf-mute until the 1st of January, 1811, would
hear and speak by the 12th.   But, as early as the
month of December, 1810, I announced the test
that I was going to make, not only to the mother of
the child, but also to Monsieur and Madame
Servier, with whom she lived, and to several other
persons whom it is needless to name.

"Very good.   But then why not make your
case more authentic?"

What do you mean by more authentic?   It
seems to me that it is sufficiently so.

"Not at all.   You must call to your experiment the *École de Médecine*, or at least a commission from the *Institut de France*, so as to have
a report in the regular way, drawn up by authorities of the art."

Authorities of what art?   Of the art of healing
congenital deaf-mutes?   I do not know such
authorities, and besides my purpose is not to
obtain a patent of invention.   What I have done,
I have done without personal interest, for the good
of science alone, and moved by philosophical
motives.   I have not wished to commercialize
my talent nor above all to enrich myself by healing
deaf-mutes.   My design has been to awaken the

attention of savants and physicians upon this subject so that they might conceive its possibility and doubt the resources of nature less. The authenticity is well enough established for those who care to see it. The opinion of others matters not to me.

"And why? But perhaps you have not reflected sufficiently. Do you know, in the present state of things, what would be the means of uniting all opinions, of establishing the authenticity of your cure, and even of making an immense fortune?"

Yes, I can divine it. It would be to heal another deaf-mute.

"Precisely."

This means would not however be so efficacious as you appear to think; for as a skeptic can never be convinced by anything, if he is faithful to the principles of skepticism, and as he is always in the right in asking the reason of the reason that one gives him, he could ask of me a third cure to prove the second, and a fourth to prove the third. It would be necessary to cure all the deaf-mutes presented to me, even those in whom the organ, lacking or destroyed, would leave no possibility of healing. A single one rejected would overthrow the edifice raised by all the others. My life would be wasted in the midst of consultations and drugs. It is true that, amid all this commotion, I might be able to make a fortune. But if, in order to devote myself to the study of ancient philosophy, I have abandoned an occupation that was tranquil and honourable, I do not see why I should take up a profession so turbulent and so far removed from my tastes. I am undoubtedly poor, but my voluntary poverty is worth more than wealth acquired at such a price.

"Then it will be said that you would try in vain to heal another deaf-mute and that the cure you have made is the effect of a happy chance."

One may say what he will. But whether the cure performed upon Rodolphe Grivel is the effect of chance or of science, it remains none the less steadfast, fixed to the goal that I meant to attain, and useful for the future solution of the metaphysical problem with which I have been occupied. A second cure would add nothing to the real force of the first; and if I heal another deaf-mute, I can state in advance that I shall do so, not because I shall believe myself forced by anything, but because my will or Providence shall have led me.

"Well and good; but has suffering humanity no rights over your heart? And if you really possess the talent of healing deafness, ought you not to give humanity the benefit of this talent?"

Yes, undoubtedly I ought to; and I hope indeed to prove to humanity that I know how to pay my debts. But, if you please, do not use words without understanding them, and do not confuse ideas. Man, always inclined to see in himself the centre of the Universe, and to believe that nature suffers when he suffers, puts his particular interest above all interests, and restricts in himself alone the whole of humanity. He demands, in the name of humanity, that he be helped when he is in peril, without considering whether the particular good that can be done for him in this case, does not comprise the general good. If one refuse him an individual service, and give preference to the world rather than to him, he cries out against injustice, inhumanity, hardness. What matters it to him that order be overthrown, that a great good be compromised, provided he be delivered from a little evil! Does he see any

of these things? A deaf person feels only his
deafness, as a miserable one feels only his misery.

Let us make a comparison.   There exist unfortunately many poor persons; and poverty, when it
is extreme, is undoubtedly an evil.   Here is, however, a man who, at first without fortune, succeeds
by dint of care and mental labours in massing a
considerable wealth. Ought he in good faith to
distribute it to those who, stagnating in ignorance
and idleness, have made no kind of effort to come
out from their condition; or who, acting contrari-
wise, have taken neither reason nor virtue as guide
in their conduct? Assuredly he should not; for,
although wishing to help them all, he would only
be able to procure for each a very transient com-
fort, and he would only plunge them afterward
into more and more misery by encouraging their
idleness.   There is not one of these poor persons
who would not believe himself right in making
demands upon this wealth, in the name of humanity, of which he creates himself the representative, and who would not be irritated when it was
refused him. If opinion on the one hand and
repressive laws on the other were not opposed
to the attempts of the timid or the audacious, it

is very certain that they would try to injure this
rich man by word or violence, and despoil the
merciless one who does not wish to give over the
fruit of his labours to them. They would take
his life perhaps, in qualifying him as inhuman.
Yet, animated by a true spirit of humanity, this
wise man might be occupied day and night seeking the means for preventing poverty in its source,
by showing its causes, by teaching how to combat them, and finally by placing his fortune in
such a manner as to serve as support for a great
number of industrious poor, many of whom, instructed by his example, might attain the same
goal.

Although every comparison fails in some points,
this one is exact enough. If I may liken myself to
a man enriched by his labours, and give to my
attainments, whatever they may be, the name of
riches, the persons who have presumed to force
me to give my riches to them, or who, upon my
refusal, have unblushingly taken vengeance in
calumnies, resemble not a little those wretched
ones who, never wishing to work, presume nevertheless to despoil those who do work.

"Admitting, according to your comparison,

that you cannot or ought not, in effect, to heal all the deaf-mutes, why at least not heal a certain number; first to assure the efficacy and authenticity of your remedy, then to close the mouth of calumny?"

You return to the same point by a detour. The efficacy of my remedy is adequately assured by the healing of Rodolphe; and I have already replied that no one can know better than I the degree of authenticity that I ought to give to this healing. For myself, I find this degree sufficient, and so sufficient that I challenge attack otherwise than by diatribes or quodlibets. And as to the calumny you suggest I evade by healing a certain number of deaf-mutes, you are very much mistaken in believing that I should evade it by that means. For, tell me the ones that should be chosen: the rich? it would be said that a base interest led me; the poor? it would be said that I corrupted them. In whatever manner I should conduct myself, those who were not preferred would have the right to complain, and cry out against the injustice. If once I began, I should be undone; and I should have only the hope of acquiring some money and much hatred, some fuss and much ennui.

"Very well! give your remedy to the public; this would be the means of evading the ̄difficulties you fear."

That is my intention, but I can only give it with certain precautions; for there could arise from its publicity other difficulties somewhat grave.

"How?"

Hear me, and permit me again to make a comparison. Supposing that in fabricating a glass in a certain fashion and with certain materials, I had come to invent a telescope by means of which I could render ineffectual a somewhat thick opacity, so as to carry my sight two or three feet underground (as did a certain Greek whose name I have forgotten), or see, for example, through a thick wall.

Such a telescope, as can easily be conceived, would be very useful in a great number of instances, and in the hands of wise and virtuous men, could render great services to society. But also to what a host of abuses could it open the door! For what perfidious uses would not the wicked and the rascally be able to employ it! Far from showing to the masses the mechanism of such an instrument, would it not be prudent, on the contrary, to hide it from them? Now, without this being precisely the case with my remedy, it would still not be good for everyone to possess it. Furthermore, everyone shall not possess it, I assure you. I promise only to strain every nerve so that enlightened men, friends of virtue and incapable of abusing a secret of nature, may attain it without too much hard work. I have already shed enough light in the letters which are about to follow; I shall continue in my other works to fulfill my promise, by pointing out the paths that must be followed.

I would that the true savants might accord me some confidence. Their approbation and esteem are more to me than great riches. I would that the government under which I have the happiness of living, might deign to approve of my conduct. No one knows better than I of what importance it is to be obedient to the laws. No one reveres more than I the monarch whom God in His wisdom has given us.

PRELIMINARY EXPLANATIONS

(2ND EDITION, 1819)

PRELIMINARY EXPLANATIONS

(2ND EDITION, 1819)

WHEN I published the first edition of these *Notions sur le Sens de l'Ouïe* and when, to confirm the letter of M. Lombard, inserted in *la Gazette de France* of March 3rd, 1811, I announced openly the good fortune that I had had of procuring the power of hearing and speech for young Rodolphe Grivel, congenital deaf-mute, Napoleon was reigning over France and over a great part of Europe. The éclat of his victories, which no reverse had yet tarnished, concealed somewhat his mistakes in politics and in administration, so that even very trained eyes could not perceive them. It was the moment of the greatest triumph of this extraordinary man, born to dazzle the world and to ravage it, and to exhaust, at the same time, the admiration and contempt of Europe. He had, at Tilsit, deceived Emperor Alexander himself, the autocrat of all the Russias; and the successor of

the Cæsars had just named him his son-in-law.
Nothing seemed left to resist him.

I was acquainted with Napoleon. I knew that
he would not allow anything extraordinary outside of himself; and, as it has been very well
known since Madame de Staël,* any sort of glory
independent of his own, was unendurable to him.
From the time of his accession to the Consulate,
astonished at some of my ideas which were new
to him, he was resolved to ruin me; and indeed,
at the first favourable occasion, he involved me
in a decree of proscription and threw me into
prison, in company with two hundred unfortunates
whom I did not know and to whom I was perfectly
unknown. He would have sent me to perish as
they did upon the desert shores of Africa, if Providence had not visibly opposed his malice. I can
only wonder at the means It employed to elude
the acts of fury of this tyrant, and bless from the
depths of my heart the generous instrument It
employed to effect my deliverance.†

---

* In her *Considérations sur la Revolution française.*

† It was M. le comte Lenoir de la Roche, at that time senator and
today a peer of France. He knew me but slightly when he rendered
me this important service. May his modesty pardon my gratitude
in this public homage that I offer to his virtues. He answered for me

It would be straying too far from my subject to explain here the secret reasons why Napoleon, without any official suit, without being aroused by any report of his ministers, did of his own accord condemn me to deportation; condemn me, a peaceful man of letters, who had passed through the Revolution without filling any direct or indirect position, and who, although known by the opposed parties through certain means and a certain strength of mind, had been equally respected. The development of these reasons will be more suitable in another work, in which I shall return to it. All that it is important to make understood now is that Napoleon hated me personally, that I knew it, and that one of two things was necessary for me to do in view of the enormous disproportion of our physical forces,—either to leave the country of his domination, which was impossible, considering the state of my fortune, or to dissimulate with him. Therefore I dissimulated, but honourably; I quietly left the literary and polemic career in which I was engaged, and I devoted myself, as much through taste as through necessity,

---

at the risk of his own head. He could do that; but how was he led to do it?

to the study of Oriental tongues and the archæological sciences connected therewith. I remained for twelve years alone, shut up in my study, without other society than my books, my wife and my children. Work became my occupation and my relaxation; fourteen hours a day were insufficient for the ardour which devoured me. I made some progress in human knowledge, I acquired some erudition; the Oriental traditions became familiar to me. It is not surprising. Man overcomes everything with will and constancy, and I was not wanting in these qualities. It was to this perseverance in my work that allusion was made by one of my old friends, a member of the *Institut de France,* in a report made to his class some years ago.*

Throughout the time of my scientific seclusion, Napoleon never lost sight of me. I saw him with his eyes fixed upon me, ready to profit by my slightest mistake, my slightest hazardous step, ready to strike again the blow that had failed, and precipitate me hopelessly into the abyss from which I had escaped only by a miracle. I took

* Delisle de Sales, author of *la Philosophie de la Nature.* It was Guinguené who gave an account of it in his annual report.

great care to be cautious; for, besides that interest which nature commands each man to attach to his preservation when the sacrifice of his life cannot be of any usefulness to the general good, I had to add to my own interest that of my family, of whom I was the sole support. I had accepted from General Bernadotte, today (1819) King of Sweden, but at that time Minister of War under the Directorate, a mediocre position in his office. Quite insignificant as was this position, I saw clearly that it disturbed Napoleon, by the purposeless bickerings he stirred up against me there, especially when the disgrace of General Marescot left me without protectors, to the attacks of his subalterns. Everything about me became the subject of observation and epilogue. I was unable to write a line without the most minute criticism being applied to sift its meaning. Twice I was nearly involved in serious trouble for having, through indignation or fatigue, allowed a weak mark of my character to escape: the first time, for refusing to write out against a commendable soldier a decree of dismissal, in illegal form and in insulting terms which Napoleon himself had dictated; and the second time, for abstaining, in the correspondence of the Minister with one of the generals-in-chief of the Spanish army, from treating as scoundrels and brigands the Spaniards legitimately armed for the defense of their country.   This last altercation, for which I was summoned before the *secrétaire général du Ministre,* might have had very grave consequences had not the one who then held this office heard my reasons with the calm of a wise administrator and felt them with the sagacity of an honest man.   But at last, as my situation became more and more difficult, I felt the necessity of sacrificing my position.   It was, however, my only means of support, and I had at that time no other resources for maintaining my family and subsisting myself.*

Nevertheless, I did not hesitate; I even saw in this event a means that Providence had reserved for me to give all of my time to study, devoting to it every moment that an irksome duty had until then snatched from it.

I therefore asked for and obtained my retirement from the *Ministre de la Guerre.*   I must say

* This position brought me in three thousand francs a year, first in the *Bureau du personnel du Génie,* and afterward in that of the *Opérations militaire.*

here, in order to render homage to the truth as
well as to the honour of the Duc de Feltre, that
he did all he could to dissuade me from this purpose. He called me into his cabinet and talked
to me for a long time in a friendly manner; but
seeing my resolution unshakable, he caused my
pension to be settled in strictly legal limits, without listening to any of the malicious chicanery
that ill-will did not fail to suggest to him in order
to hold me under the yoke I wished to break.

This modest pension and three months salary
that the Duc de Feltre accorded me as gratuity,
testifying that my leaving his offices was voluntary on my part, furnished me with the necessary
means and time to provide for the needs of my
family. Already, foreseeing from afar this catas-
trophe, and profitting by certain economies and
certain favourable circumstances which presented
themselves, I had arranged for my wife to enter
an institution for young ladies, as proprietor of the
establishment and associate in its administration.
The knowledge my wife had acquired upon the
subject of education, of which she had made a
thorough study, her talents, and her virtues were
not long in imparting to the institution confided

to her cares and to those of Madame Servier, a value which, in assuring her success, sheltered me for some time from any kind of apprehension.*

Although these details may at first appear foreign to the subject with which we are occupied, I feel, however, that I should make them known, in order to give the reader the facility of understanding things which, without their assistance, would remain inexplicable. In the first edition of this work I could not touch upon them in any manner whatsoever; and that is why so many obscurities were found in it. The principal point is, as I have said, the personal animosity that Napoleon bore toward me; an animosity terrible and irreconcilable, the motives of which only he and I could understand and appreciate. My position was critical to the highest degree in his eyes, and I needed a singular prudence to escape from the snares he continually set for me.

To tell the truth I must say that this animosity of which I speak, which I have qualified as irreconcilable, had not always seemed to me such. Nat-

* My wife remained in this establishment, as proprietor and associate, until the second entrance of the allies into Paris, in 1815. Since
that time it has been under the exclusive care of Madame Servier.

urally remote from hateful passions and the bale-
ful effects that they cause, I had for quite a long
time believed that Napoleon would return to more
just sentiments regarding me. Although I knew
very well that in everything concerning moral
and religious ideas the son of the Corsican Bonaparte was only a very ordinary and even a very
puny man, I could not deny the fact that as poli-
tician and above all as warrior, nature had endowed
him with very distinguished talents. I saw his
mind inwardly, half black and half white, of darkness and of light; so that certain qualities, being
constantly enlightened, amazed one by the per-
manency of their éclat and seemed to gain in gran-
deur as one regarded them; whereas the other
qualities, always plunged in gloomy darkness, remained inert, and by their shallowness and their
immobility escaped the inattentive glance, or
else repelled the eyes firm enough to consider
them. I had made several attempts to induce
the light into the dark part of his being, and to
bring him back to the morality and justice from
which his steps had turned him, the more so as
these steps were all convulsive and gigantic. My
efforts were in vain and his hatred, which I had

believed weakened by time, showed itself visibly more implacable than ever. Therefore I found myself still obliged to dissimulate, to evade a storm I was not in condition to sustain. I wrote absolutely nothing for him directly; but I also wrote nothing against him. When I was forced by circumstances to do so, I praised the praiseworthy qualities which all the world praised, and I was silent concerning the others. I wrote some trivial verses, and to lull to sleep the dragon whose piercing glance spied upon all my movements, I insinuated certain complimentary phrases into the works I wanted to have printed. I knew too well that without this nothing proceeding from my pen would see the light of day under his reign. Thus it was, that on the occasion of his coronation, I could not refuse the request of the *Consistoire de l'Église reformée de Paris*, for an Oratorio of which I wrote the words and the music;* that I yielded to the entreaties of a celebrated painter who had exhibited Napoleon's portrait in enamel in the Salon, and composed some stanzas in which, through praises somewhat obscure, I

* The manuscript of this Oratorio is now in the possession of the *Bibliothèque de la Société de l'Histoire de Protestantisme Français. Tr.*

had the adroitness to give him a very strong lesson
if he sensed it; that in publishing my eumolpic
translation and my examinations of *les Vers Dorés
de Pythagore*,* I addressed to him a flattering com-
pliment upon his warlike inspiration; and finally
that in presenting the first edition of these *Notions
sur le Sens de l'Ouïe* and venturing to make public
the phenomenon that I had performed in develop-
ing this sense in a congenital deaf-mute, I endeavoured to cajole his bad temper by ascribing the glory
to him.

I was not duped as to the effect all this produced upon him. I knew unquestionably that
his irritation was increased by it, and that where
others saw respect, he saw only irony. But the
wrath of a tyrant is ludicrous when it is powerless.
In reality I cared nothing for a resentment which
he was unable to show, and with a sort of pride I
saw him stamping upon my works to stifle them,
ordering all his menials to do the same, and using
thus his hatred and his strength to no purpose;
for I knew that he would pass, he and all the sup-
porters of his tyranny, and that my writings, which
he could indeed repress, but never sully, would

* *The Golden Verses of Pythagoras.* Putnam, N. Y.

remain long after he had passed away. What he did in regard to my work upon *les Vers Dorés* is truly ludicrous. I shall give an account of it in a second edition, in which I shall omit the parasitic phrases that referred to him, as well as correct certain errors that slipped into the first edition. I must limit myself here with what came to pass concerning *Notions sur le Sens de l'Ouïe*.

In the first place, I pray the reader to assure himself that I attribute, voluntarily and with positive knowledge, the ridiculous persecutions that I have experienced in consequence of this work, not to the persons who have executed them directly, but to the bizarre man who instigated them indirectly. These persons were not free; they could only obey the terrible influence that moved them. I should be unjust in my turn, if I did not distinguish between the cruel hand that held the instrument, and the instrument itself. There are, among these subservient ones, many in whom I recognize eminent virtues, and many others whose minds and talents I should be the first to praise.

There is no enlightened man, a just appreciator of events, who does not feel of what importance is the development of the sense of hearing in a congenital deaf-mute, for the benefit of natural and moral sciences as well as for the welfare of humanity in general. The reader, therefore, will doubtless permit me to turn back a little, so as to surround the fact of this healing with all the proofs possible, by reason and by evidence.

I have said, in beginning these *Explanations*, that the hatred of Napoleon, which was manifested against me in the first year of his Consulate by a decree of proscription from which I escaped only by a remarkable kindness of Providence, forced me into a sort of scientific seclusion for more than twelve years. This interval of time which I consecrated to study, could not be entirely lost. When I withdrew from a literary career, I was not without some learning. I had explored with certain profit the literature of Europe, the principal tongues of which I spoke quite fluently. I threw myself eagerly upon those of Africa and of Asia; and it may be, according to the expression of doctor Gall, that nature has favoured me with the philological faculty, for it is certain that in a few years I studied a great number of idioms and penetrated their genius. I then conceived the plan of writing the history of the earth, an enormous plan,

perhaps above the strength of a man to achieve.
But I followed it with activity, clearing ancient
sterile tracts of tradition in order to compare the
different cosmogonies of the principal nations of
the globe. I had already compared those of the
Chinese, Tibetans, Hindus and Parsees, when proceeding thus, in spirit, from the orient to the
occident of Asia, I came upon the cosmogony of
the Hebrews, which we call vulgarly, *Genesis*. At
that time I was familiar with the Hebraic tongue
but as it was taught in the universities; that is to
say, I knew how to give to the Hebrew word the
meaning adopted by the Hellenists in the version
called the *Septuagint*. But I was not long in perceiving that this meaning was worthless; that the
Essenian Jews, to whom Ptolemy the king had
confided the translation of the books of Moses, had
fooled him.

Fortified with the learning I had drawn from
my previous researches, I began to study Hebrew
with an indefatigable ardour; and without concerning myself in any manner with either Greek or
Latin, I probed the roots of this ancient idiom with
adequate force and constancy to divest them of the
mire which had enveloped them, and to bring them

up again, as it were, to the surface of the ground.
I examined them, and as soon as they were sufficiently understood by me, I resolved to reëstablish upon them, as upon its veritable bases, the
edifice of the Hebraic tongue, fallen away for more
than twenty-four centuries. I made a new grammar, I made a new radical vocabulary, and I
translated, according to my new principles, the
first ten chapters of the Sepher, supporting this
translation with all the proofs that the comparison
of the idioms analogous to the Hebrew,—the
Samaritan, the Chaldaic, the Syriac, the Arabic,
etc.—could furnish me.

This work, in two volumes *in-quarto*, was terminated toward the end of the year 1810. But
to have written it was not all. It was necessary
to have it printed; and would Napoleon consent
to this? I tried to sound him by a flattering letter, which, despite the obstacles he had raised so
that nothing of mine should reach him, came to
him, nevertheless, by a very extraordinary course,
and roused his curiosity. He threw my letter in
the fire after having read it; and although I begged
him earnestly to reply to me yes or no, he did not
reply either the one or the other. As he was

at that time extremely occupied both with his
divorce from Josephine and with his new alliance,
as well as with preparations for the war which he
already planned against Russia, I ventured to profit by his distractions and emerge for a moment
from my seclusion. Making use of the common
proverb, *He who says nothing consents*, I resolved
to take his silence as a tacit assent, and to present myself to the Minister of the Interior.

A friend of mine, M. R—— P——, then one of
the pastors of the *Église reformée de Paris*, charged
himself with my introduction to M. de Montalivet, who held the portfolio. He explained to
him in few words the object of my visit. This
Minister, struck with the immensity of my work,
received me with much distinction. He listened
to what I said to him upon the Hebraic tongue,
upon the possibility of its restoration, and understood perfectly the incalculable advantage that
the physical and moral sciences might derive from
a new translation of the Cosmogony of Moses,
constructed upon unimpeachable grammatical
principles, and more appropriate to the enlightenment of the century. I had several long confer-
ences with him, in one of which I read to him the

Introductory Dissertation which stands at the
head of my work. He appeared disposed to have
it all printed at the expense of the government and
I beheld the moment when I was about to have
quite an advantage over Napoleon. But unfortunately M. de Montalivet had more sagacity than
force of mind; his reflections destroyed the work
of his thought. He feared, with some appearance
of reason, that Napoleon might be angry that he
had made, without sanction, a decision so important. When I again saw him, he limited himself
to the offer of printing half my work; that is to say,
the grammar and the radical vocabulary, holding
back the translation of the Cosmogony of Moses
with the relative notes thereof. I had not reck-
oned on this. The danger remained the same for
me, without any advantage to compensate me.
Consequently this Minister saw me refuse his offer
with a spontaneity and firmness to which he was
little accustomed, and which nettled him. A
somewhat lively discussion took place between us,
out of which sprang the first thought which led
me to develop the sense of hearing in a congenital
deaf-mute; and this is what happened.

As I was speaking earnestly of the sublime beau-

ties contained in the Sepher, and as I was telling
M. de Montalivet, what I have since published,
that this ancient book, having issued complete
from the sanctuaries of Thebes and Memphis,
contains all the secrets of the Egyptian priesthood,
and develops, in few pages, the principles of all
the sciences, the Minister stopped me brusquely,
and said: "Monsieur d'Olivet, if what you advance with so much energy be true, if the principles of all the sciences are in the Sepher, you
ought to know them, since you flatter yourself
with having restored the tongue of this sacred
book, and since you have translated ten chapters of
it. Very well. Demonstrate for me a single one
of these principles and I will have the whole of
your book printed."

Struck with this argument, and perhaps a little
nettled in my turn at the kind of challenge thrown
at me, I replied to the Minister that I would do
what he asked me to do, and I went away.

There was, at that time, in the institution of
M. l'abbé Sicard, a young man named Rodolphe
Grivel, about fifteen years of age, born at Aubonne
in Switzerland, and a congenital deaf-mute. This
young man, endowed with much intelligence,

had made quite good progress in the understanding of signs during the six years that he had passed with M. l'abbé Sicard, so that this able instructor had often taken pleasure in having him appear in public exercises. He belonged to a very distinguished family from the canton of Vaud, and at Paris had relatives well known in the financial world. By a singular coincidence, his mother, then a widow and having only this child, determining to come to Paris so as to be near him, and wishing to profit by her stay here, had accepted a place as *sous maîtresse* in the *pensionnat de jeunes demoiselles* which my wife managed jointly with Madame Servier. I had several times seen young Rodolphe when he was visiting his mother, and I was as affected by his natural infirmity as I was touched by his happy disposition. In the position in which I found myself, it seemed to me, as it still seems to me, that Providence placed him in my path to give me occasion to reply victoriously to the challenge of Napoleon's minister, by applying to this deaf-mute the principle of a science that I well understood, and certainly the one of all which is found the most clearly expressed in the first ten chapters of the Sepher, when one knows how to read them.   Who would not have felt as I did?

Rodolphe Grivel was not an obscure child whose origin presented doubts.   His relatives occupied a high rank in the canton of Vaud.   From the time of his birth they had tried every means to cure him of an infirmity which all the physicians agreed was innate and incurable.*   For six years he lived at the *Institution des Sourds-Muets;* he was raised and educated there at the expense of the government; all Paris knew him, having seen him appear at the public exercises.   What more authentic could one desire?

I took advantage of the New Year vacation to persuade Madame Grivel to retain her son with her for several days, and I proposed to her the bold experiment I was contemplating.   She consented to try it; and as it will be seen in the letters to my friend wherein I give account of this event, the auditive organ, inert with Rodolphe Grivel, having received life on the 9th of January, 1811, gave unequivocal marks of audition on the 12th of the same month, and continued to develop, by successively admitting and classifying all sounds,

* See *Documentary Proofs,* No. 1.   Page 177.

from the lowest to the highest. I pass over the progress of this development, so as not to repeat what I shall say further on, and I hasten to show the result of my experiment.

Following the consecrated custom of the Protestant religion, and particularly of the Swiss who profess this religion, Madame Grivel, convinced that the natural infirmity of her son existed no longer, publicly rendered thanksgiving to God on Sunday the 3rd of February, by the voice of M. Rabaud, officiating pastor.

A young man named Lombard, struck with what he had heard, hastened to see me the following day to know the facts of this phenomenon, was convinced of their truth, and as happens at the age still exempt from prejudices, became enthusiastic. He wrote a letter* upon this subject which was printed in the *Journal de Paris*, and in the *Gazette de France* on the 3rd of the following March. Thus the affair acquired publicity. A great number of persons came to me to offer felicitations. M. l'abbé Sicard was by no means one of the late-comers. He came on the 9th and on the 15th of March; the first time accompanied

* See page 231.

by several persons who were unknown to me, and the last time alone. He appeared as much satisfied as surprised at the phenomenon offered to his observation, especially on his second visit. Then he congratulated me with emotion, congratulated his former pupil and Madame Grivel, talked with me for a long time, and embraced us all with a great outpouring of the heart. M. Lombard was present; and Rodolphe, whom I had accustomed to keep a journal of all that concerned him, has given an account of this touching scene with great ingenuousness.*

Everything appeared to go according to my desires. I doubted not that my book would soon be printed. But my illusion was not of long duration.

M. R—— P—— who had gone triumphantly to see the Minister of the Interior to give him an account of this event, and to claim the performance of his promise to me, returned very sad. "Monsieur Fabre d'Olivet is ruined," said the Minister to him, approaching with a melancholy air. "The Emperor has seen the article inserted about him in the *Journal de Paris*, and has shown great temper. There is nothing further to do."

* See *Documentary Proofs*, No. 2. Page 182.

I felt it only too keenly.   Moreover, for I knew
the Emperor, I saw that I was to be the object of
persecution.   The mistake, if it was one, was committed; I could not draw back, I could only try
to avert the storm by manœuvring; this was what
I did.

Compelled to renounce for the time being the
project of having my work printed, I desired at
least that the means which I had attempted to
attain this end, and which had failed, might serve
for something useful, in throwing new light upon
the origin of speech and upon the manner by
which the ideas are attached to the signs which
represent them.   Consequently, I directed all my
observations from this side, and I arranged so
that my pupil should so direct his.   The journal
of his thoughts which I possess, and which forms
quite a large volume, contains things very remarkable on this subject.   In the meantime I hastened
to publish the *Letters* that I had written to one of
my boyhood friends, who, by singular chance had
known Rodolphe's father at the college of Mühl-
hausen, where they had been students together,
and was bound to him in quite a close friendship.
In order to reassure Napoleon as to my subsequent

intentions and to calm his wrath, I stated positively in my *Preliminary Notice* that I renounced the course I had begun and that I would not undertake to give hearing to other deaf-mutes. I believed by this compliance to ease his mind and induce him to leave me alone; I was mistaken.

The journals which at first were eager to spread abroad my discovery, closed themselves to my friends, and opened only to the sarcasms that my enemies poured down upon me. My study, in which I had at first seen several judicious and impartial observers, was filled only with spies and detractors. In the midst of this tumult I remained calm, I did not reply to the quodlibets, and I let them laugh as much as they liked, the malicious and the silly. So far, the anger of Napoleon was lost in smoke. He saw it, and being unable to arouse my vanity, laid a trap for my kindheartedness into which I allowed myself to fall

I had made it clearly understood, even as I am about to relate, that my intention was not to undertake any new cures; and for a long time it was in vain that any one tried to shake my resolution, even with most brilliant offers. But at

last, a difficult circumstance presented itself. A
friend and compatriot of Rodolphe Grivel, named
Louis Veillard, also congenital deaf-mute, being
convinced of the truth of the phenomenon I had
performed, took it into his head to be likewise healed of his infirmity. This young man,
more than twenty years of age, had keen imag-
ination and ardent feelings. Whether he acted
really of himself, or whether, as I have thought
since, he was inadvertently forced, he began to
pursue me with a constancy that nothing could
repulse. He wrote to me, he obliged me to write
to him, he came to see me, he implored me, he
wept. At first all was useless; but what he was
unable to do with me, he could do with persons
to whom I was held by ties strong enough to com-
pel me to refuse nothing. These persons, touched
and circumvented, urged me many times and to
such a degree that I yielded. Nevertheless, Louis
Veillard was not entirely free. He was dependent
upon an engraver of precious stones, a member of
the *Institut de France*, with whom he was appren-
ticed. Undoubtedly there was nothing so simple
as to ask his master for him for a few days. I did
not believe that he would refuse. But as I was

not acquainted with M. J——, he might think that my good intention arose from self-interest; and it seemed better to entrust a person of an analogous profession, Mlle. R——, a distinguished pupil of M. Isabey, to propose Veillard's coming to a private house to model a portrait in wax. This portrait was of me. It was not the first portrait that Veillard had executed outside his master's house; and I think it would certainly be admitted that this innocent ruse, used moreover for a purpose so praiseworthy, did not merit for Mlle. R——, sister of an officer, a general in the Russian service, the threat of a lawsuit. This was, however, what happened.

But before pursuing this singular story, I must repeat here what I have already said: that it is not to the persons who are found implicated in this affair that I attribute the unjust persecutions I have experienced, but in reality to Napoleon alone, who made them act, often unwittingly.

Thus then, Louis Veillard, brought to me to model my portrait in wax, did, in truth, model it. The price agreed upon was offered to his master, who refused it. It is true that something not agreed upon with him was executed at the same time and that in the space of several days, his pupil received from me the faculty of hearing and speaking. The correspondence of this young man, from the midst of the torments and terrors with which he was surrounded during sundry months, proves this fact irresistibly.* And should one ask me how it could be that having received this faculty, he does not, however, possess it to-day, I should answer that he has lost it through lack of cultivation and development.

Let the spirit of routine which attaches itself to the grossest errors be laid aside for a moment, and let it be seen that the faculty of hearing is not audition, nor is the faculty of speech, speech itself. A new-born infant brings these two faculties into the world, but does it hear and does it speak? Does it even see, although it may have the faculty of seeing? No. It must, for a long time, exercise these faculties so that they pass from power into action. Must noises and sounds not enter insensibly into its ear, and there be classified, as rays of light bring images of objects to the eyes? What labour has the infant's vocal organ not had before being able, following the impulse of will, to utter an articulate sound and to attach a meaning thereto!

That which is lacking in the ear of a deaf-mute is life. Life can be established there, and awaken the dormant auditive faculty; but cultivation and care must aid its development, otherwise life will again become extinct therein, and with it the awakened faculty. What happened to Veillard was inevitable; lack of experience and reflection prevented my realizing it at that moment; but time has taught me. I experienced the same disadvantage with Marie Rolland.* This young girl, for whom I had developed the auditive faculty, as I had for Veillard, being surrounded with superstitious terrors and deprived of care, has in like manner lost this faculty. Of seven individuals to whom I have had the good fortune to give hearing, two have thus allowed it to escape, whereas the other five, objects of the assiduous care of wise parents and intelligent teachers, have developed this faculty, have retained it and have made rapid progress in the exercise of speech. But without anticipating

* She lives at St. Hippolyte du Gard; I shall speak of her at greater length further on.

events any further, let us see, in a few words, what transpired in regard to Veillard.

Hardly was the Imperial government informed that I had given or intended to give audition to a second deaf-mute, than it was thoroughly aroused, so violent was the impulse Napoleon had given it against me. It seemed that I had committed a crime of *lèse-majesté,* and that offended humanity demanded my punishment. In a few days I was summoned five times by the *préfet de police,* interrogated as a criminal and treated in the most merciless manner. I was threatened with a warrant; but at the moment of issuing it, a sentiment of justice, stronger than all the authority of the tyrant, arrested the pen of the magistrate. This magistrate, whose intelligence and integrity I have had good cause to appreciate since, visibly feigned an indignation he did not feel. Realizing this, I recall that in the midst of a very heated discourse, in which he endeavoured to prove to me the enormity of my fault, I interrupted him to say coldly: "The words which come out of your mouth are not in your heart, *Monsieur le préfet,* and what you say you do not believe."

In the course of this singular affair I had good

reason to perceive that tyranny is never complete in a nation that has a public opinion; for this opinion envelops the agents of the tyrant and the tyrant himself, and prevents the former from understanding the orders which are not clearly expressed, and does not permit the latter to express them clearly. Napoleon was only the expression of a military tyranny. Also his authority was only complete when his armies could be moved, and where they had significance. He needed great spaces to display his strength. Wherever his soldiers were unable to penetrate, his power was weak and almost insignificant. He has been foolishly compared to Robespierre. They were exactly opposite, the one from the other. The latter, who can be regarded as the expression of a popular tyranny, was reflected in the smallest revolutionary committees. No public opinion existed save his. Those who had the misfortune to place reliance elsewhere were lost. The narrower the space, the stronger he was. In great spaces he could do nothing. Also this subaltern tyrant fell as soon as the circle of his authority was extended and he wished to move great masses. The contrary happened to Napoleon; in proportion as the

space contracted he felt his strength diminish, and
this colossus could no longer breathe when the
atmosphere of Europe began to fail him.

If in the position in which I was, I had had to
deal with Robespierre, I should not have been able
to escape being the victim of his ferocity. One
single oblique glance confided to one of his hired
assassins would have determined my downfall;
but Napoleon, who hated me enough perhaps to
desire it, could not achieve it by a crime. He
needed to have motives, at least specious, to make
the judges take action; and he had none. Also
all this great scandal terminated in a manner quite
ridiculous for him. His Minister of the Interior
named a commission, as I understand it, to examine the important phenomenon of which I have
just given the first examples in Rodolphe Grivel
and in Louis Veillard. I say, as I understand it,
for this minister did not give me any information
in this regard, and did not name any of the persons who composed his commission. I received a
letter, quite insignificant, from M. l'abbé Sicard,
in which he told me that this committee would be
composed of savants and would meet at his home.
I replied in the same tone, giving him to under-

stand that I did not find myself legally convoked by him, and that I would not go.

The commission acted therefore as it wished. No statement, no official report was submitted to me. I did not know and still do not know what were its operations. What I certainly do know is, that Rodolphe Grivel, who ought to have been the principal subject of the examination of these savants, was not called in. They decided on his account without seeing him, without questioning him, without hearing him; he was judged by default, upon the sole deposition of a single witness, strongly to be challenged, since he was also a judge; Rodolphe was charged with and convicted of never having been deaf and dumb, whereas it was known that he had remained during six years as such, in the house of the instructor of deaf-mutes himself, at the expense of the government.

Thus this powerful Napoleon who did not wish me to give hearing and speech to a congenital deaf-mute, found, in order to destroy the authentic fact of my having done so, only false material with which to oppose me. This he caused to be printed in *le Moniteur*, and spread throughout

Europe by means of the journals of his hirelings. However, before trying this ignoble method, he wanted to be assured of my silence; for he knew well that I could easily break it, and that I should undoubtedly break it, if I had before me only the members of the commission.

He made me appear again before the *préfet de police*, who, after having declared to me, on the part of the Minister of the Interior, that the intention of His Majesty was that I should meddle no more, directly or indirectly, with the healing of deaf-mutes, asked me if I was ready to obey.* It would have been more than foolhardy to reply negatively to such a demand. I did not have fifty legions at my command. I answered therefore that I deemed the order compulsory and that I would obey.

I must remark that in notifying me of this extraordinary order, the *préfet* was troubled. The injustice that he found himself forced to do me appeared revolting to him. He showed it by the warm-hearted and conspicuous manner with which

* This order was delivered verbally. I made several attempts to obtain it in writing, so as to have a rather odd monument to the tyranny of Napoleon; but never did I succeed in obtaining it. My letters on this subject all remained unanswered.

he conducted me through the crowd which filled his antechamber, among whom were several persons who were there only to observe my demeanour and perhaps his. When we were at the door of the stairway, he said to me these words which I have never forgotten: "Monsieur d'Olivet, I am not in sympathy with all this, and such would not have been my decision. One must abide one's time."

Some days later, Veillard was sent to Geneva, without my being permitted either to see him or to speak with him; and when it was well assured that I was attempting no move, the famous report of the commission was allowed to appear, in which it was stated that the Rodolphe Grivel whom I had pretended to heal of congenital deafness had heard and spoken from the age of four years.

The family of the young man was shocked by this assertion, and its justifiable resentment was shared by all the local authorities, by all the notable inhabitants of the canton of Vaud, and even of Geneva, who had known Rodolphe. As it was unknown whence the stroke came, and as, instead of the Imperial hand, one saw only the instrument he used, legal proofs and the most authentic certificates were hastily sent to me, in order to overthrow the false material and to annul the report. But my promise bound me, and I preserved them in my portfolio, without making any use of them. I "abided my time," according to the expression of the *préfet*.

The time was not as long as might be imagined.   All this happened toward the beginning of 1812, and in the first months of 1814 the tottering colossus fell, raised himself by a convulsive movement in 1815, and soon fell again never to rise.   I was then entirely absorbed with the printing of my work upon *la Langue hébraïque restitutée;** I could not be diverted from it.   But as soon as I saw myself free from cares, and saw that a wise and paternal government offered me a guarantee of the laws which it has itself accorded to the just liberty of the press, I determined to publish these documents, which prove irresistibly the congenital deafness of Rodolphe Grivel and also designate him authentically deaf-mute from birth, as well as the legitimate son of his father and mother.†

It can be seen in glancing through these proofs,

---

* *The Hebraic Tongue Restored*, Putnam, N. Y.
† See *Documentary Proofs*, No. 1, 4 and 5.   Pages 177, 188 and 189.

that there is no other means of verifying the civil facts, and one cannot call them in question without overthrowing society. I have added an extract from the letter of M. Corver-Hooft, who belongs to one of the first families of Holland, and who, at the time of this affair, was chamberlain of Napoleon.* M. Corver-Hooft, indignant over the turn given to this affair, and having no idea of the part taken by the Emperor, offered at first to speak to him about it; but as he considered it prudent to sound the Minister of the Interior, he was not long in perceiving that he could do nothing, and that the hatred of which I was the victim had another source than that which the masses believed.

After these explanations, which were indispensable, I pass on to the letters to my friend. I have omitted the first letter, as I did in the first edition, because it offers only an abridged repetition of what has just been read.

* No. 6, page 192. This letter was given me by M. le colonel Gordon, to whom it was addressed, with the permission to print it when circumstances permitted.

LETTERS

LETTERS

LETTER I

NOTE. This letter having been almost entirely given in the Preliminary Notice, I am leaving it out to avoid useless repetitions, and substituting the reply made to it, which served as occasion for the letters following.*

Ferrier to Fabre d'Olivet

GANGES, February 11th, 1811.

I HAVE read with the keenest interest, *Monsieur et cher ami*, your letter of January 31st. You obtain from your long labours a fruit so much the sweeter since you did not seek it in the beginning. A profound and intelligent study has given you this fruit with many others.

The second birth of Rodolphe interests me so much the more since I was the friend and companion in study of his father, since I had the intimate knowledge of his condition of muteness and deafness, and since I knew the daily sacrifice made

* See Note 1, page 155.

65

by his mother to procure for him the instruction of M. Sicard. This event interests me furthermore because you have produced it, and because the bond of friendship which has united us from childhood, attaches me also to your welfare and your success.

Your letter leaves me no doubt as to the verity of the event; no one, in my place, would experience the least uncertainty. I know the child, I know that he was a congenital deaf-mute; I know your frankness, your virtues, your strict probity; I am convinced. But, my dear friend, prepare yourself to fight sarcasm, disparagement, calumny. All men have not, as I have, determinative motives of conviction; many even would repulse them if they had them. Be that as it may, go forward with firm step to your goal; heal Rodolphe, present him to your slanderers and the truth will triumph.

If the assurance of the stand that I am taking in this extraordinary event be pleasing to you, I can at least give you this satisfaction. Also, having been deeply impressed with the state of isolation and of death in which the son of my old friend languished, I can tell you that I envy in a way

the happiness you must enjoy, after having procured for him a new existence.

Add to your first communication the details of
events which may follow and you will give me thus
a new proof of your friendship; you will procure
me the pleasure of testifying publicly my private conviction, and of converting some incredulous ones. *Adieu, Monsieur et cher ami;* work
for the welfare of men, it assures your own.

FERRIER.

P. S. Extend my felicitations to Madame
Grivel; she experiences a happiness above all
expression. Poignant as the sorrow of losing a
cherished son, so must be the joy of seeing him
reborn at fifteen years of age. Do not forget that
I shall be exceedingly eager to receive your news.

LETTER II

Fabre d'Olivet to Ferrier

PARIS, March 10th, 1811.

I SHOULD have liked to give you sooner the
details that you have asked of me, *Monsieur et
bon ami;* but numerous occupations have put
obstacles in the way of my good will. The son

of your old friend Grivel, whose healing I announced to you, continues to make rapid progress in the classification of sounds and in the comprehension of ideas attached to them, in considering them as signs representative of thoughts. But it is not upon the specific work of this child that I wish to speak to you today; I will do so in another letter. I wish to acquaint you with the motives which urged me to make this extraordinary cure, the end that I proposed, and the general effect that it has produced.

I will begin with its effect. When for the first time an unusual thing strikes the attention of men, one can judge of the force of their reflection and the measure of their knowledge by the effect it produces upon them. Now, this is what I have remarked: at the first rumour noised abroad that *hearing* [ouïe] had been given to a congenital deaf-mute, and that this deaf-mute *heard* [entendait], most persons, misled by the double meaning of the word *hear* [entendre], foolishly imagined that this deaf-mute *comprehended* [comprenait] and that they could abruptly propose to him the most singular questions. Astonished to see him insensible to their discourses, remaining unmoved and mute, regarding them with a troubled air, they have often judged that he did not hear them, which was assuredly true in a sense. Other persons, more thoughtful, justly separating audition from comprehension, have not committed this error. They have plainly felt that *to hear* [ouïr] sounds is neither to grasp them nor to classify them, nor even yet to comprehend them; and that it is necessary for a deaf-mute to pass through all the phases of audition, of distinction and of classification, to arrive at comprehension; that otherwise he is no more than a stranger among us, an Iroquois, an extraordinary being, a man fallen from the moon.

I cannot say which of these two classes of persons has been the more numerous; what is certain is, that a very decided line of demarcation has separated them. Among the former have been those who, even after having seen Rodolphe, have doubted his healing; among the latter, those who, before having seen him, judged his healing impossible. In examining the first of these classes I have been convinced of the ascendancy that words assume over minds, and the grave errors into which their abuse can lead. I have discovered a poverty in the French tongue, and I have regretted the loss of the verb *to hear* [ouïr], which has not been replaced. In examining the second class, I have recognized the force of prejudice, the pride of knowledge, and the sorry usage that has been made of the word *impossible*, the effect of which has been to dispense with the study of nature and belief in Providence.

This is the general effect. As to my motives and my goal, you will find them indicated strongly enough in a letter I have written to a mother of two children, congenital deaf-mutes, who petitioned me to give them hearing as I had given it to Rodolphe. I add here a complete copy of this letter.

Adieu, *Monsieur et bon ami;* and believe in my very sincere friendship.

FABRE D'OLIVET.

Fabre d'Olivet to Madame B—— R——

MADAME,

The letter that you have done me the honour to write, bears the impress of two sentiments, the

* See Note 2, page 155.

expression of which I have marked with attention. The first, and the more salient, is that of a tender mother, who eagerly seizes the hope of giving to her children a faculty which nature has refused them; the second, and the more involved, is that of an intelligent person doubting a thing of which the truth is not demonstrated to her, but which, however, would be precious to her. These two sentiments are natural, and are only praiseworthy. Although you may not be entirely convinced of the healing of Rodolphe Grivel, none the less you petition for the healing of your two children, congenitally deaf-mute as he was; for after all your tenderness sees, in trying the test, only a happy chance for them. I pray you, Madame, to give me a moment's attention.

I am not a physician; I have not sought, in making an extraordinary cure, to invite notice, or to give myself what is called a clientele. I do not wish to practise medicine. I do not compose any kind of elixir or opiate that can be sold. I am a man of letters. Known in my youth by somewhat unimportant productions, I have long since discontinued these more frivolous forms of literature. I am applying myself to the study of ancient philosophy, and I have already delved considerably into the deep but little explored mine of Oriental traditions. It is from this source that, returning with certain knowledge unfamiliar to the moderns, I have seen the savant world disagree upon points of the highest importance: sometimes it is the origin of the earth and its place in the universe that divides the philosophers, sometimes it is the birth of man and the principle of speech that occupies the thinkers. One asks himself whence ideas come: whether they are innate in the intelligence, or produced by sensation. Hosts of difficult questions are agitated of which I am sparing you the useless nomenclature. The book of Moses, which ought to have decided the first question, is written in a tongue lost for twenty-five centuries; the translations are obscure and insufficient, the commentaries prolific and uncertain. A persistent study, aided by certain favourable circumstances, revealed this tongue to me. I saw Hebrew under a new light; I worked unremittingly to restore it. I composed a grammar and a dictionary; I translated the first ten chapters of Moses, and I re-established the cosmogony of this extraordinary

man. Then an unexpected revelation dawned
upon me. But how should I propagate this revelation? Who would be my guarantee? Who
would decide among the contending sects of philosophy? I dared to try a bold experiment; I
felt that the greatest difficulty was connected
with the metaphysics of language, and that if
one had clear ideas of the formation of ideas, he
would be quite near to understanding them.
Providence, for I must call It by Its name, sent
to me young Grivel, a congenital deaf-mute, fifteen years of age, full of intelligence, and very
advanced in the acquisition of signs through the
efforts of M. Sicard. I felt that in giving him
audition and comprehension, I would make of
him an unusual man, who, carried suddenly into
a new sphere, would there mature the knowledge
of the old sphere, and might in time unveil to us
a multitude of mysteries upon the origin of thought,
and its liaison with the signs that represent it.

Pardon, Madame, this long digression. It was
necessary in order to explain to you the motives of
a healing that some are not only content to deny,
but seek also to corrupt in its principle. On this
occasion I have acted as philosopher and not as

physician. If Rodolphe hears and speaks, he will certainly know one day how to treat his slanderers as they deserve. As for me, my task is fulfilled. Averse to notoriety, I would have kept silent concerning the experiment I made, if the child who was the subject had not been, by providential circumstances, in the public eye. It was necessary that his fifteen years of deafness and muteness should be sheltered from every attack, in order that a certain ascendancy in philosophy be obtained.

Now I believe, Madame, that I hear you repeating the phrases of your letter, and saying to me that, devoting myself to studies so useful to humanity, I ought not to refuse to employ my curative means in favour of other deaf-mutes who demand them. The good of humanity is undoubtedly the object of my studies, but, Madame, do you think that deafness is the sole evil with which humanity is afflicted? Without considering blindness and countless other physical maladies, what of moral blindness and deafness? Do you think that the many pretended savants who are attacked by it have no need of remedies? They believe they know the world, and they do not know themselves; with balance in hand, they weigh Saturn and his satellites, and are ignorant of how to calculate the life of a gnat; they make systems upon the flood and ebb tides of the ocean, and know not by what law the sap rises in plants; they establish a mechanism of the universe and do not perceive the providential laws which involve themselves.* While Providence, unveiling Itself before their eyes, leads a triumphant hero from glory to glory, invests him with strength of will, and lays by his hands the bases of a fixed empire, they do not feel Its progress and are ever struck with the same astonishment at each step he makes.

I trust, Madame, that you will deign to appreciate the reasons which necessitate my refusing your request. I repeat to you once more that I am not a physician, but a man of letters.

If I should ever renounce the resolution I have taken to limit my attentions to the education of one single pupil, believe me, your children would be my first interest. However, my cosmogonical works will undoubtedly be printed, and everyone may be able to draw therefrom the

* See Note 3, page 156.

same knowledge and the same curative means.* Rodolphe Grivel himself should be able one day to devote himself to the education and relief of deaf-mutes. Even now he is so far advanced in the two languages, that he could successfully fol- low the instruction of any pupils afflicted with deafness who might be confided to Madame Servier, in whose boarding school his mother is a teacher. I myself could guide his lessons. This is all that I can promise.

Deign to accept, Madame, my respectful salu- tations.

FABRE D'OLIVET.

LETTER III

Fabre d'Olivet to Ferrier

PARIS, April 8th, 1811.

AFTER having stated, as I told you, *Monsieur et bon ami*, in my letter to Madame B—— R—— (which was inserted in the *Gazette de France* of March 15th), the motives of the bold experiment I attempted upon Rodolphe Grivel and my pur- pose in healing this young man, its results

* See Note 4, page 156.

must be examined. I will endeavour to do so with simplicity, as briefly as possible and without leaving my philosophical precincts. It will be necessary to pardon certain divagations in the phrases, certain neologisms in the terms, for time presses me too much to shorten my style further, and the subject is too new for me not to be forced sometimes to leave the academic circle.

Three months have hardly passed since the auditive faculty was given to Rodolphe Grivel, and this young man begins already to comprehend articulated language, and to make use of it to express his ideas. To judge matters rigorously it seems that he ought to be, relative to this language, only about what a child of three months would be; for it is well enough known that when one is deaf from birth, being necessarily mute, it is only from the moment when he begins to understand that he is really able to aspire to speak. But it must be taken into consideration that this child was fifteen years old when he was born to speak, that his intelligence had been developed by a laborious study, that he already knew the use of signs, and that his first expressions were a translation of a written language into articulate language; therefore his course has been infinitely more rapid. It has been so rapid, that a man of merit, a good observer, present recently at one of his lessons, told me that if the savants did not hurry to see him, they would run the risk of finding him no longer either dumb or deaf. This, however, is a philosophical hyperbole; for whatever may be said of his disposition to hear, his deafness was too complete and his vocal organs were too rusty by fifteen years of immobility for the infirmity from which I have fortunately delivered him, not to have left profound traces. Neither time nor practice of speech will probably ever entirely efface them.*

Perhaps I ought to have retarded his progress. But he was too eager to attain the development of his faculties for me to think of opposing his advance; and besides I felt too much the necessity of imposing silence upon calumny, which, contradicting itself, would then assert that he had never heard, as it asserts at present that he heard beforehand. All it was possible for me to do was to accumulate experiments. I did not let any circumstance escape from which I might draw

* See Note 5, page 157.

some light. First I opened a journal of my observations; and as soon as my pupil found himself in condition to comprehend what I wished to say to him, I taught him to open a journal for himself, in order to record his observations therein. One cannot imagine what a mass of interesting things his journal contains, all crude as it is, and of what value it will one day be to Rodolphe, when, enlightened by speech and moulded by intercourse with people, he wishes to review his primitive ideas and go back to the time of his silence and his isolation. I shall sometimes have occasion to quote this work, unique in its kind, and I shall always quote his own expressions. I know very well that the world will not hesitate to attribute it to me. But what can be done? Have I the means of verifying its authenticity? Would any precautions reassure those who everywhere see only sterility of nature and absence of virtue?

In the midst of these observations and these numerous experiments that occasions have brought forth, and that I have classified without keeping other order than the one of time, you see how difficult it would be to proceed by a rigorous analysis. It is by reflecting upon their general effect that I have been able to form a system, and every system presents itself to the mind under synthetic form. I am about to try, my friend, to acquaint you with this system, such as I have deduced it from facts offered to me in the exploration of a phenomenon as new as interesting.

I conceive, attached to each of our senses, to distinguish, conserve or modify their diverse impressions, three principal faculties: *attention, memory* and *judgment;* and three secondary faculties: *reflection, method* and *comprehension.* The attention perceives by reflection; memory classifies by method; judgment is exercised by comprehension. These six faculties develop *sentiment,* which is to *sensation,* their common base, what sensation itself is to *sensibility,* its fundamental principle. Now, in the phenomenon in question, the kind of sensation that we are about to examine is produced by the auditive faculty. This physical faculty, reacted upon by the six intellectual faculties that I have called *attention, memory* and *judgment, reflection, method* and *comprehension,* constitutes what we call hearing. In hearing there is *audition* and *understanding;* this distinction is of the greatest importance. It is by sensation that one *hears;* it is by sentiment that one *understands.* One understands only that which he has perceived by attention and reflection, distinguished by memory and method, arrested by judgment and comprehension.*

In order that a man who receives the sensation of sound have sentiment, that is to say, that he understand after having heard, it is absolutely necessary that the three operations indicated above take place. If one of them is lacking, he understands very badly that which he may hear very well. With the man accustomed from his infancy to the impression of sound, the audition does not appear different from the understanding, because the operations necessary to join the two extremes and produce hearing are executed unconsciously in an indivisible instant. But it is not the same with the man who tardily enjoys the auditive faculty, and whose intellectual faculties, for a long time strangers to this kind of sensation, are incapable of reacting to it. It is in such a case alone that one can ascertain their existence and study their important activity.

* See Note 6, page 158.

82   The Healing of Rodolphe Grivel

At the moment when young Grivel enjoyed for the first time the auditive faculty, his intellectual faculties had, for fifteen years, been ignorant of its existence; their agitation was strange to him and they were a long time without producing the sentiment of hearing or the understanding of sounds. After having lost consciousness for a few moments, he recovered himself only to fall into a sort of stupor from which it was quite difficult to arouse him; and I had, with his mother and the persons witnessing my experiment, the unusual spectacle of a child who felt noise without grasping it, and who heard without understanding.*

I shall tell you, *Monsieur et bon ami*, in what manner this first experiment was made; and the theory I have just established I shall support upon proofs *de facto*, which experience has provided for me, giving you an account of what you wished to know, in a series of letters similar to this one. I hope that they may appear to you as interesting as you expected them to be.

I renew the assurance of my inviolable friendship.

FABRE D'OLIVET.

* See Note 7, page 158.

LETTER IV

Fabre d'Olivet to Ferrier

PARIS, April 10th, 1811.

LET us return for a moment to the way in which I conceive *sensation* to be developed by means of the six intellectual faculties that transform it into *sentiment*. This theory of the senses is perhaps new enough to merit, *Monsieur et bon ami*, a moment of your attention. I shall, for more clarity, present the system to you under the form of a geometrical figure. Let us imagine a central point; unfolding a circumference by means of a radius which, acting under six diverse modifications, is its mathematical measure. Let us consider sensation as represented by this central point; it would be to sentiment, which it develops, as the point is to its circumference; and the intellectual radius by means of which this transformation is accomplished, would be manifested under the six intellectual faculties that I have named *attention* and *reflection*, *memory* and *method*, *judgment* and *comprehension*. Thus sentiment is, as Condillac, following in the steps of Locke, has said, a sensation transformed; but its transformation, far from being a consequence of its own force, as Cabanis appears to think, must take place by means of a radius that these three philosophers have ignored. But this is neither the time nor the place for us to stop upon the laws of this transformation, to examine whether the ideas that are its necessary consequence come or do not come exclusively from the senses. It seems to me that it is well, before affirming anything upon this difficult question, to know precisely what a sense is. This is perhaps what so many philosophers who have affirmed so much, have not thought of knowing. For after all it is not in a fantastic statue, as Buffon, Charles Bonnet and Condillac have imagined, that one can study the course of nature. It is necessary to unveil nature itself to penetrate with any certainty into this important mystery. It is necessary that a congenital deaf-mute, passing from audition to understanding, consent to the analysis of hearing, that one of our senses which furnishes the most material to the intelligence, by the use of speech which is its indispensable regulator. I am not far from believing that the light this analysis will furnish, illuminating the systems of Bacon, Descartes and

Kant, may show the point of union, and put in accord these great men, whose badly criticized opinions are not so dissimilar as one believes.

My theory of the senses thus explained, let us pass on to the experiments which have suggested it to me, and which serve as proof.*

The means I employed on young Grivel the 7th, 9th, and the 11th of January prepared the auditive organ to receive the impression of sound, by reëstablishing there the seat of sensibility, or by surmounting the obstacle opposed to its action.† I had some reasons for believing in its efficacy; nevertheless, there was no exterior evidence at this time. The child, for any other but myself, seemed as deaf as he ever had been. I declared however that he was no longer deaf and I shall relate the experiment that demonstrated it.

The 12th of January, toward evening, at a moment when Rodolphe least expected it, a large copper casserole‡ was struck behind him with the big end of a stick. He was being held by the sleeve. The impression that he felt was as great as I had foreseen. He reeled, his sight

---

* See Note 8, page 158.   † See Note 9, page 158.
‡ See Note 10, page 159.

was dimmed. He fell, semi-unconscious, in the arms of his mother, who was obliged to administer vinegar to bring him back to himself.

It is evident that, from the moment when the means had worked upon the auditive organ until that in which its effect became visible, that is to say from the 9th to the 12th of January, a sort of torpor, produced by fifteen years of immobility and non-exercise, had caused the effect of a deep sleep or lethargy in the intellectual faculties of young Grivel. The sound struck his ear without finding anything there that it could arouse; sensibility, vainly excited, was a sterile point without radius and without circumference. Thus the sound died out in vacuum. So a sleeping animal has no feeling of a sting, although his quivering hide announces sensation. The intellectual faculties, put in movement by the loud clamour of the casserole, although sharply disturbed, and struck with a terror difficult to describe, obeyed nevertheless to a certain point and revealed the sentiment of the new sensation they experienced. Rodolphe heard for the first time in his life. But he did not grasp, or distinguish, or comprehend what he had heard for never before had his attention, his memory, or his judgment been exercised upon any like thing.

Without giving his shaken senses time to leave the channels of audition into which they had entered for the first time, I made him hear my voice. He understood it and testified to it by gestures. I wrote certain words; and repeating them syllable by syllable, slowly and several times, I had the pleasure of making him say quite distinctly: *I thank God; I love mama.** As he then found himself tired with the scene that had just transpired and the work he had done, he asked to go and rest. I allowed him to do so after having made him say, again under my dictation, to Madame Servier who was present: *Goodnight, Madame.*

The young man's mother, overcome to tears at having heard this *I love mama* that she had vainly awaited for fifteen years, transported with joy at having seen her son give the positive marks of audition, did not doubt that he understood perfectly. She expected that he might waken the following morning with an inexpressible delight in hearing her maternal voice, in receiving the impression of all the sounds that she judged must

* See Note 11, page 161.

be pleasant to him.   The persons present shared
her hope.   All gave vent to their natural feelings
over so extraordinary an occurrence, and confus-
ing audition and understanding, thought that
Rodolphe then and there could grasp, distinguish
and comprehend all the sounds that might strike
him.   I alone had another belief, but I took care
not to express it.

The following morning, instead of the delight
expected, the young man, on the contrary, showed
a sort of stupor.   His expression was sad and
dreamy; he hung his head and seemed to feel a
sentiment of fear.   Company worried him; he
sought to be alone.   His mother tried in vain to
draw him from his revery, by calling him, by causing noises about him; he remained immobile.
Thoroughly frightened, she came to me to relate
the incidents that disconcerted her hopes.   On
the other hand, M. Servier, in whose room Rodolphe slept, told me that early in the morning
he found him awake and seated upon his bed, a
thing that had never happened before.   He did
not doubt that he had received, perhaps without
knowing it, the impression of the bell which had
rung for the rising of the boarders.

When his mother brought him to me at the hour arranged for his daily lesson, I was not long in seeing that what had alarmed her was an effect pure and simple of the extraordinary state in which Rodolphe found himself. This child, receiving the impression of all sounds without understanding any of them, that is to say, without grasping, classifying or judging them, found himself in a situation wholly new, strange, and undefinable even to us, but painful and fatiguing to him, and from which he made useless efforts to emerge. He was called; but did he know that he was called? One clapped near him; but what was it to clap? Who had taught him to distinguish its name? Could he recognize among thousands of noises, all unknown, a noise to which his attention had never been fixed, which his memory had never retained, of which he had not appreciated either the form or the value? Relative to sound, he was what the child blind from birth was, relative to light, when healed by M. Chelsen. This one, although receiving the impression of objects, did not see them, since it was impossible for him to grasp any form or to distinguish any one thing from another, however different they might be in form and size. Rodolphe as deaf-mute, experienced also a sort of fright, which came from the nature of sound, different from that of light. The desire or the tendency to be self-absorbed explains how that deaf-mute of Chartres, to whom nature alone gave audition, far from testifying his surprise or his joy, was able, on the contrary, to conceal what he felt and to remain for a long time without telling anything of his healing to his relatives. My pupil might have acted in the same way if I had left him free; but I had very strong reasons for guiding him in another direction.

With renewed, etc.

FABRE D'OLIVET.

LETTER V

Fabre d'Olivet to Ferrier

PARIS, April 13th, 1811.

IT is certain that if, after having procured the auditive faculty for young Grivel, I had left him to himself, or if nature alone, by an unexpected crisis, had produced the effect owed to my attentions, this child would have testified nothing of his condition. He would not have been able to.

He would have carefully restrained within his
breast the emotions he felt, and like the deaf-mute
of Chartres, would have patiently waited to
understand and judge perfectly what he felt before manifesting it exteriorly. But I was there
to watch him. The control I had over him, even
before he understood his healing, did not permit
his concealing anything from me. I followed all
his movements. I saw developed, although under
other relations, the same phenomena that struck
M. Chelsen after having removed the cataract
from the eyes of the child born blind, of whom
I have spoken. This child, seeing for the first
time, was so far from being able to judge distances, forms or colours, he believed that all objects, indiscriminately, touched his eyes, as the
things he felt with his fingers touched his skin.
Objects appeared to him as a single mass, enveloping him, pressing him on all sides, offering him
only a confused *mélange*, a chaos in which it was
impossible for him to recognize anything, to distinguish anything, to comprehend anything.* My

---

* Voltaire mentions the blind child who in 1729 was operated upon
by the surgeon Chelsen or Cheselden, and adds, "All that he saw seemed
to touch his eyes." *Tr.*

young deaf-mute experienced interiorly the same
effect that the blind child experienced exteriorly.
All noises, all sounds, of whatever nature they
might be, were in him, resounding in him, making
part of his being. At first he did not conceive
of them as more foreign to his person than the
emotion they brought forth. All reached him
at once, confusedly mixed, and without his being
able in any fashion to distinguish their kind, their
volume, or the body, the place, the distance
from which they came. He sought the cause in
himself, and centred within himself more and more
according as his intellectual faculties were more
and more disturbed.*

Some believed, and his mother herself was
persuaded that he distinguished certain noises,
such as thunder, cannon, drums and wagons
rolling in the street; but it soon became evident
that they had been mistaken as to the sensation. Here is again a trait of resemblance with
the blind child. M. Chelsen states that this
child, although he could tell the difference between
day and night in the time of his blindness, and
believed he could even discern with a strong light,

* See Note 12, page 161.

black, white and bright red, did not recognize any of these colours when they were shown him after his healing, and asserted that they were not the same as those he had formerly seen. To judge clearly of Rodolphe's sensation, one must read how he expresses himself in his journal. Here are his reflections under date of March 1st:

"While I am in bed, I hear the wagons; before being healed, I did not hear them. . . . I work always in my room. When M. Fabre comes, he knocks gently at the door to make a proof of the noise upon me; then I go to open it. . . ."

"When I was deaf at M. Sicard's I believed I heard the thunder, the cannon; I was mistaken. I only felt them.* It was an internal *shuddering* which came in all my body from head to foot. The drum was the same; it was an interior *commotion*. But at present I really distinguish sounds, and I hear the noise of the objects."

The words *shuddering* and *commotion*, which are found in this last paragraph, were furnished by me; and it was in this manner. Rodolphe, having decided to express his thought, lacked the word necessary to render it. After having

---

* See Note 13, page 163.

searched for a long time in a dictionary, he came
to me with the book in hand and gave evidence of
his perplexity. I asked him to depict for me by
gesture what he wished to say. He first carried his
two hands from the soles of his feet to the top of
his head, agitating them with an undulating movement. I gave him *shuddering;* I might have given
him likewise *tremor* or *vibration*. After, he put
his hands on the pit of his stomach, shaking them
the one upon the other. I gave him *commotion*.
These two words were comprehended and approved
of by him.

But let us return to the condition in which he
was a month and a half before writing what I
have just quoted. He was, as I have told you,
Monsieur et bon ami, absorbed in himself, seeking there with good faith the cause of the new
sensation he experienced. The only means of
drawing him from this condition was to pass in
review before him a great number of sonorous
bodies, to occasion under his eyes a great quantity
of noises and of different sounds, to teach him to
judge of them and to recognize them finally, by
relating them to their types. But in what a
labyrinth was he involved! and where to begin?

what route to follow? Again I saw a striking
resemblance between the blind and the deaf child.
The former having too many objects to retain at
once, forgot the greater part; and for one thing
that he conserved, he let a thousand escape. It
was the same with the latter. In this difficulty,
I decided to act first, with regard to my pupil, as
a mother acts with regard to the child she trains.
I gave him over to nature, for the classification
of noises and of sounds that chance made him
hear in abundance, only returning to them later
for the observations to be made. I restricted
myself to teaching him, for the time, to understand the sounds produced by the vocal organ,
the numberless combinations of which serve as
material for speech.

To this end, I arranged a sort of alphabet, in
which I made a first distinction of vocal and con-
sonantal sounds as simple and compound, and a
second of these same sounds as soft, loud and
very loud, according to the vocal touch. Little
by little I accustomed Rodolphe to listen to my
voice, to grasp its inflections and to distinguish
them, in order to retain them. His intelligence,
already developed by the knowledge of signs, en-

abled him to make rapid progress. Two of his principal faculties, attention and judgment, were not long in being awakened, and in provoking reflection and comprehension; but memory was more rebellious. So long as my alphabet was before his eyes, he did not hesitate to follow my voice; he imitated even the most fleeting and most delicate inflections. But as soon as this support was lacking, he fell into an inexpressible trouble. An *a* struck him as an *o*, an *e* as an *i;* he confused *u* with *ou*. If I pronounced *ba*, his memory furnished him with *pa*, *fa*, or *va;* he understood *cha* for *ja*, *ja* for *za*, *ta* for *da*, *ra* for *la*, the sibilance of the *s* appeared to him insurmountably difficult to retain.*

One cannot form an idea of the strange fluctuation that sounds underwent in his ear. For us, with whom the memory of sounds has been insensibly formed since infancy, the sounds seem retained as soon as grasped; but this is an error of habit. There is nothing so difficult. Rodolphe, whose auditive faculty has been exercised for three months, who hears and speaks very well for this time, who is beginning even to play

* See Note 14, page 164.

the piano, cannot yet conceive how one can keep an *air* in his head, that is to say, a series of sounds to which no determined meaning is attached. Every time he hears singing, he asks where the music is. All my efforts to make him comprehend the manner by which singing is accomplished have been useless. As his memorative faculty does not know how to furnish him with two sounds one after another, he does not suspect that there exist musical memories that can retain not only various songs and all kinds of melody and harmony, but even symphonies for large orchestras and entire operas. His incredulity on this point has furnished me with the innocent proof that it is indeed difficult to accord to others, or even to conceive in them, a faculty in which one himself is lacking.

Despite this difficulty, which is inherent in nature, and that which comes from a vocal organ rusted by fifteen years of inactivity, young Grivel was not long in grasping all the inflections of the voice, in uniting them in syllables, and grouping the syllables so as to form words. I put him to reading, and I began making him write certain easy phrases under my dictation. M. Servier, for whose kind care and zeal I am exceedingly grateful, aided me in this work, by making my pupil repeat the lessons that I had given him.

At last his mother, an assiduous witness to his progress, and as pious as tender, seeing him near to attaining the usage of speech for himself, did not wish to delay further giving thanks to God for a healing that she regarded as a boon of Providence. She wrote to the pastor, who came to see her, and was convinced by his own eyes of the phenomenon for which she begged him to render thanksgiving publicly. On the 3rd of February, Rodolphe Grivel, congenital deaf-mute, was presented by his mother at the Protestant Temple, and there uttered, under dictation, this prayer, which M. Lombard has quoted: *I thank God for having given me hearing and speech.**

With my renewed, etc.

FABRE D'OLIVET.

LETTER VI

Fabre d'Olivet to Ferrier

PARIS, April 15th, 1811.

I HAVE tried in my preceding letters, *Monsieur et bon ami,* to make you acquainted with the

* See Note 15, page 164.

manner in which I conceive the sense of hearing to be produced in us, according to the observations I have been able to make upon young Grivel. But up to this point it has only been a question of the interior system, that is to say, of the mode of the transformation of sensation into sentiment, or, what is the same thing, of the difference that should be made between simple audition and the understanding of sounds. I have not spoken of the exterior system, that is to say of the sound in itself, and of the organ that receives it. I believe, however, that I ought to explain to you my thought upon this subject, especially since the experiments permitted me by an extraordinary phenomenon have furnished me with illumination concerning the nature of sound and the conformation of the ear, that your sagacity will doubtless find worthy of attention.

I shall not dwell upon the vocal organ. Its defect produces only an accidental dumbness, often easy to cure, and however persistent it may be, influences the intelligence but little. A mute who is not deaf can, through hearing, acquire as many ideas as other men; whereas one born deaf, instructed to simulate speech by mechanical

means, remains none the less a stranger to general
and abstract ideas.   For only by speech can their
germ fecundate in him.

I know in history two famous examples of persons born dumb, who, not being deaf, have spoken
suddenly on important occasions.   One concerns
the son of Crœsus whose story is known to all the
world, thanks to Herodotus who has related it.
This prince, as you know, seeing a soldier about
to strike his father without recognizing him, experienced so violent a desire to express the terror
with which he was seized, that his tongue, until
that moment impeded, became loosed all at once,
and he cried out: "Stop, soldier, it is the king!"

The other example, much less known, concerns
an athlete, named Æglea, who was present at the
sacred games in Samos.   He owed the faculty of
speaking to the keen indignation with which he
was moved when seeing the trickery of the one
who drew lots for those who were to contend in
the games, in which he himself was to be one of the
actors.   Aulus Gellius relates that in his rage he
cried out: "I saw you do it."

I likewise know of two examples of deaf-mutes
who have acquired the faculty of hearing.   The

first is the one of whom I spoke, the deaf-mute of Chartres, who, according to what one reads in the volume of the *Académie des Sciences* for the year 1703, began suddenly to speak, to the great astonishment of the whole town. The second is a young man in England, who received the auditive faculty through a crisis occasioned in his brain by a violent attack of fever. The deaf-mute of Chartres, born in the lower class, deprived of instruction, repressed within himself all the emotions he experienced, and was unable to furnish any light upon the phenomenon of which he was the subject. Questioned by theologians, instead of by physicians or philosophers, he never even thought of giving reasons for the diverse impressions that sounds made upon his ear. As to the young Englishman who emerged from delirium to enjoy a new faculty, I do not know whether he was in condition to make the analysis. The tome of *Transactions philosophiques*, in which I read the report, is no longer at hand; and when I read it, I did not realize the need that I might have for it one day.

The vocal organ of Rodolphe Grivel, although lacking in flexibility and greatly impeded by long dumbness, has no notable defects. I have said that on the same day when this young man heard, he spoke; that is to say, he was able to imitate certain words that I dictated slowly to him, and to repeat them after me.* The greatest difficulty he experiences is not owing to organic construction, but to the habit he had acquired of submitting to mechanical means to give forth certain sounds. The pressure that was practised upon his throat has given him a sort of guttural *o*, which returns constantly despite himself, and which I doubt he will ever succeed in throwing off completely. His ear is well formed, interiorly as well as exteriorly. It is upon the ear that my experiments have been directed, since I have hoped to profit by the occasion offered me to understand sound in itself and the manner by which it affects our auditive organ.

However, although I only sought, as I have said, to make him understand vocal inflections, and although I left to chance the care of presenting indirectly to him other sounds and less important noises, chance and his own curiosity have served me quite well. Hardly had the month of February passed before he had himself classified a great many things. It was even observable that he

* See Note 16, page 164.

would be endowed with quite a talent for imitation. He mimicked the crowing of the cock and the clucking of the hen wonderfully; he barked with the dog, mewed with the cat, knew how to reproduce the discordant tone of the donkey passing in the street; the cries of the milkman and the water-carrier were familiar to him. He loved to make noise, whether with his foot or hand. He heard, as a curious thing, his fingers drumming upon a table or upon the window-pane. He mumbled unformed words between his teeth when he thought himself unobserved, and stopped abruptly as soon as he saw that he was noticed.*

During the first days after his healing, before he had his own room in my apartment, he would go up to the garret, and all alone there, would practise repeating the words I had taught him, or would teach himself new ones. He was careful not to practise in the garden; for not yet possessing an exact measure of hearing, he imagined that all the neighbours could hear him from as far as they could see him.† He took much pleasure in music. One evening M. Servier played the flute while I accompanied on the cello to see

* See Note 17, page 164.   † See Note 18, page 166.

what effect this harmony would make upon him. He seemed very sensible to the deep tones of my instrument; and when I had finished, he silently took it and passed into the anteroom. There, alone in a corner, he set himself to draw frightful sounds from the cello, making the bow shriek upon the strings, which he scraped with all his might. Madame Servier, who arrived in the midst of this din, interrupted it to ask him what he was doing. He understood her very well and replied without much hesitation: *I am amusing myself.**

This was the first indication I had that deep sounds pleased him most, and were better heard by him than high sounds. A second experiment confirmed me in this idea.

I took him, on the Thursday before Lent, to a small party where many children were gathered with young ladies to amuse them. M. Servier obligingly played the violin. There was dancing, singing, and much noise in general. Rodolphe, to whom I had suggested that he give me an account of his sensations, wrote the following morning in his journal: "Thursday, the 21st of February, the young ladies, being disguised, danced.

* See Note 19, page 166.

While they sang, M. Fabre asked me if I could distinguish their voices. I replied to him that they were not exactly alike, and that that of M. Servier was more pleasing to my ears."

In the midst of a very noisy singing game, being desirous of ascertaining whether he began to grasp the ensemble of the voices, and whether he distinguished that of the person who sang the refrain, I asked him, and he proved to me that he distinguished it very well. Turning his face to the wall, he indicated by a gesture the moment when this person ceased singing or began again.* He informed me then that the voices had differences so great for him that he could not believe the words they uttered belonged to the same language. When I asked him what voice he liked the best, he told me without hesitation that it was mine, next that of M. Servier, and then that of his mother. The voices of young persons, and especially those of children had much less attraction for him, and often seemed disagreeable.

I noticed, as soon as he could tell the difference between sounds and noises, that *noises*, that is to say, those sensations of the hearing not appreci-

* See Note 20, page 167.

able according to harmonic laws, struck him more directly, and awakened his intellectual faculties sooner. They pleased him more than *sounds*, properly speaking, that is to say, those sensations produced by bodies, the regular vibrations of which exhibit a more homogeneous contexture. The denser the sonorous body, the quicker its vibrations; so that the more sonorous it was, the less he grasped its vibration. The dull noise of wood struck in any manner whatsoever, the slightest collision of two inharmonic bodies, the least cracking, seemed louder to his ear and left a more durable impress than the more resounding sounds of crystal, of silver or of copper. When these latter sounds were made very near him, or when they resulted from a very sharp blow, they fatigued him and ended by hurting him.* Here is what he wrote on this subject: "Friday, March 8th, M. Fabre wanted to know if I heard a bottle that was struck with a knife, a shield with another; I replied to him that I believed I heard them. M. Fabre told me that the sound of glass is sharp and resounding. It pained me a little; it hurt my ears. M. Fabre told me also that the noise of silver is

* See Note 21, page 168

clear, acute and resounding. It seemed to me
cutting and it *roughs* my throat.* . . .

I perceive, *Monsieur et bon ami*, that this
letter is lengthening out too much, and is passing the limits I have set myself. I am obliged to
put off until the next the sequence of these details.

With renewed, etc.

FABRE D'OLIVET.

LETTER VII

Fabre d'Olivet to Ferrier

PARIS, April 18th, 1811.

Here, *Monsieur et bon ami*, is the sequence of
what Rodolphe wrote pertaining to the effect of
different sounds: "I hear," he continues, "the
paper on the wall of the salon better than the red
cup that is struck with the little spoon; this aston-
ishes me. M. Fabre told me that the sound of
the cup is resounding, and that of the wood is dull.
The sound of the clock is like that of the cup.
M. Fabre plays the violin. He told me that the
heavy strings give low sounds, and the thin strings

* See Note 22, page 168.

high sounds. I always find that the low sounds are the most agreeable to my ears."

It is important to say that when I made this distinction to Rodolphe, he had much trouble in understanding me. He was unable to conceive that we should call *low* the sounds that seemed to him loud and which he heard wonderfully; and *high*, on the contrary, the sounds that he hardly heard because of their tenuity. If I had left him to his own ideas upon this point, it is certain that he would have classed the musical scale according to the system of the ancient Greeks, and that he, as they, would have called *descending* what we call today *ascending*. As to the verb *rough*, which is the invention of this youth, and which I left in my preceding letter with scrupulous exactitude, he himself gave me its explanation by replacing it further on with *scraping*. The sound of silver, he told me, scraped his throat disagreeably; and he added that other sounds sometimes affected him in the region of the stomach or the heart, sometimes at the top of the head, sometimes in the teeth, sometimes throughout the whole body. Undoubtedly it so happens to most of us, in spite of our being accustomed to it, when we hear the filing of a saw, the polishing of marble, or the scraping of glass.* The only thing of which he could not give me an idea, since he lacked absolutely the word to express it, was the effect he felt from the sustained sounds of an harmonica. He tried however to depict it, by joining his two hands above his head and moving them in a circle around it, as if he wished to draw an aureole, or give me to understand that he was as though enveloped in a sonorous sphere.

But, without insisting further upon particular experiments, let us glance rapidly over the general progress that the auditive faculty of young Grivel followed in its development. In establishing the great division of sounds and noises, we see that noises were the first to be seized and classified. In considering noises, as J. J. Rousseau conceived them and as I conceive them, as the sum of a multitude of diverse sounds being heard at once and reciprocally provoking their undulations in some manner, we see that the first noises within reach of Rodolphe were the ones which were the least homogeneous, the dullest, the most divided in their essence. In considering sounds as being

* See Note 23, page 169.

of a nature more and more harmonic, in proportion as the body producing them is more elastic, more homogeneous, and formed of a substance the degree of purity and cohesion of which is more perfect and more equal, we see that the last sounds to be heard were the most resounding, the sharpest, those resulting from the greatest number of vibrations.

Thus it can be concluded that a body is noisier the more it is divided into unequal masses of solidity and of contexture, and more sonorous the nearer it approaches to homogeneity.

It also seems, according to the numerous experiments that I have made upon Rodolphe's ear as this organ has been developed in him, that the hearing of man is first opened to noise; and that passing insensibly from inharmonic to harmonic, or from diversity to unity, it arrives at sound.* Now the lowest sound the ear can grasp, according to Euler, is that which results from a body furnishing twenty vibrations per second; and the highest sound, that rendered by a body, the number of vibrations of which rises to four thousand in the same space of time. Rodolphe who hears

* See Note 24, page 169.

all noises, is still far from hearing all sounds. At the end of three months of practice, this is about the point at which he finds himself:

He hears, in a well-closed room, the exterior noises, whatever they may be, to which the human ear is accessible; and in the street he distinguishes a cart from a wagon or a cabriolet very well. In his journal he says, "M. Fabre asked me what the carriage was when it passed in the street. I indicated it well, and I indicated it by saying that a carriage is moving, it is going quite quickly and it is pleasing to my ears; that a cart goes very heavily like the turtles, and that a cabriolet goes lightly and by jerks. . . ." As to sounds, he grasps them at various distances, according as they are more or less analogous with noise. The sound of a drum is the one that he hears best of all. I have moved back of him to more than two hundred paces, striking a child's drum, without his ceasing to give signs of audition. A small bell, a crystal glass or a porcelain cup has to be struck at less than six feet from his ears for the sound rendered to be sensible to him. The flageolet affects him at nearly the same distance; the flute, at two or three times the distance, according to

the high or low tone; the violin, in the same proportion but farther away than the flute; and the
cello, in the same relation to the violin. I have
not tried the bass-viol, but I am persuaded that
it would act following the same laws.

It is worthy of attention to notice a *Mémoire*
that I have received from Milan, concerning
the condition of a person completely deaf, who
believed that I was a medical man, and asked for
a consultation. It tells me that this person, whose
accidental deafness began to manifest itself at
the age of twenty, lost first the highest sounds,
then the medium, and finally ceased from grasping
the lowest, hearing only certain dull noises. Thus
the gradual course of the loss has been exactly the
inverse of the acquisition.

After this data of which you will easily see the
importance, *Monsieur et bon ami*, let us pursue our
exploration, and see by what manner sound com-
ports itself exteriorly, relative to air, its indispensable vehicle. I say indispensable; for although it
appears sometimes that water, liquids and even
solid bodies may transmit sound, it can be supposed that this transmission may take place by
favour of the air contained in these fluids or these

bodies, as has been demonstrated in the *Mémoires de l'Académie* for the year 1743.

All physicists know that sound experiences sensible alterations from the air in which it is maintained and that it becomes stronger or weaker, is carried to more or less considerable distances, according to the state of this fluid. They plainly prove that it is weaker in proportion as one rises above the level of the sea, and stronger in proportion as one descends into deep regions where the air is more compressed. They show that a bell, enclosed in the receptacle of a pneumatic machine, ceases wholly to make itself heard; its sound becomes fainter in proportion as the vacuum is made. From this, they conclude rightly that sound is always proportional to the density of the air, and that it augments and extends by direct reason of this same density.

These same physicists, led by the analogies that they observe between light and sound, teach that sound is propagated in a straight line, and they give echoes, regarded as sonorous reflections, as proof of their assertions. But here the proof *de facto* abandons them, and I have very strong reasons for believing that they are mistaken in this point. I think, on the contrary, with the celebrated Bacon, that if the impressions of visible objects are made by straight lines, those of objects sensible to hearing are made by curved lines. One can see what this savant observer has written on the subject in his *Sylva Sylvarum*. He teaches there, with a rare sagacity, that luminous rays and sonorous vibrations are carried from the centre to the circumference, following the whole extent of a sphere the sonorous or luminous body of which occupies the centre, but exercising their action in different ways; light, by infusing therein, so to speak, its own nature; and sound, by impressing its particular movement. Very far from the modern physicists, who, however, call themselves his disciples, Bacon thinks that light and sound have nothing of the material. He states, on the contrary, that the bodies which dispense them spread no corporeal effluvium which might fill their orbit or sphere of activity, but only certain immaterial forms or species, which, penetrating without being divided, act in an inverse sense without one obstructing the other.

I feel that one might extend very much this theory of sound, but as this is not a treatise on

physics that I am writing, it is needless for us
to dwell upon it further. I must proceed rapidly.
After having examined sound, relative to the subject which occupies me, in the body that produces it and in the medium that transmits it, it
is necessary to consider it in the organ that receives
its impressions.

With renewed, etc.

FABRE D'OLIVET.

LETTER VIII

Fabre d'Olivet to Ferrier

PARIS, April 22nd, 1811.

THE ear being the organ endowed with auditory
faculty, naturalists and physicists, curious to
know in what manner the sensation of hearing is
operated by its means, have studied to understand it; more perhaps than medical men, who,
despairing of healing its infirmities, which are
too hidden from their eyes, have not meditated
sufficiently upon its structure. My intention is
not, *Monsieur et bon ami*, to enter into long ana-
tomical details, which are foreign to these letters,
and in which, moreover, I am little versed. I will
continue to proceed rapidly in order to arrive at

certain new conclusions that my experiments have put me within reach of obtaining.

The ear, properly speaking, or that part of the organ which is shown exteriorly, is only a sort of funnel, destined to receive the ambient air disturbed by sonorous vibrations. Its shaft, called the *auditory canal*, terminates with a thin membrane that is named the *tympanum*. Behind this membrane the interior ear begins; and it is the sole essential for hearing, since the conch-shell exterior may be entirely lacking, and even the tympanum be destroyed without the hearing suffering a noticeable weakness. Even the ossicles that are found behind this tympanum, and that have been named quite improperly *malleus*, *incus* and *stapes*, through the supposition of their having analogous functions, appear to be of little importance. For persons in whom they were decayed have been able to hear, and it is known that birds, whose hearing is very good, do not have them at all.

The interior ear is composed of the *caisse* of the tympanum, hollowed out of the bony part of the temporal bone, and of what is called the labyrinth, placed behind this cavity. This cavity, as Buffon has very well observed, appears to be only for echo, where sound, carried by the auditory canal, is reflected. The tympanum, which has been wrongly considered as a drum destined to receive certain vibrations and to communicate them to the ossicles, is in reality only a partition. It is placed by nature at the entrance of the temporal cavity to prevent any outside thing from altering its structure, or harming the echo that is formed therein; for the sensation of hearing is only an echo, a sonorous reflection, as that of sight is only a luminous reflection. The labyrinth communicates with the temporal cavity by a membranous cavity still more interior, called the *vestibule*. From one side of this vestibule go three semi-circular canals, interlacing each other in the manner of a hunting-horn; on the other side is the spiral, which is regarded as the principal constituent of the auditory system. It is a kind of tube turning spirally around a core of a slightly flat conical form. The cavity of this tube diminishes gradually in approaching the top of the cone, and is divided throughout its length in two halves called *ramps*, distinguished as external ramp and internal ramp, by a partition named *osseus lamina*, of which one portion is bony and the other membranous.

Now let us remember that the commotions or vibrations communicated to the air by the collision of bodies or by their resonance, are propagated in this fluid from the centre to the circumference, following the extent of a hollow sphere of which these bodies occupy the centre. To give a perceptible picture, it is almost as we see pebbles, falling into the water, forming circles that extend with more or less force and quickness, according to the specific weight of these bodies. The movement impressed upon the air is developed with an astonishing speed, and ceases to make itself felt with like rapidity. Every voice, every sound is born and dies almost at the same instant. For example, let a person, being in an open place, make his voice heard. At once the ambient air is stirred around him; the sound reverberates, is propagated from the centre to the circumference, and disturbs from place to place, in less than a second of time, a hollow sphere of more than a thousand feet in radius. At the extremities of this sphere, and in its interior, one distinguishes the most delicate nuances of the voice, of which every one of the articulations is found complete in every part of the air. The air thus disturbed, gathered in by the auricular shell, follows the auditory canal as far as the tympanum which it passes through in order to make echo in the temporal cavity. There it executes the first act of audition. This act is more or less perfect, according to the disposition of the place and of the air which fills it.

It is known by the experiments of Bacon that sound is reflected in a manner inverse to that of light. Whereas light is reflected in a mirror, and forms a picture so much the more exact as the mirror is more polished, sound has need of encountering a hollow place, the cavity of which must have certain proportions, to make echo and send back a just repetition of itself. The echo of sound, as the original sound, is propagated circularly in the air that modifies it. It is more or less strong, more or less clear, following the state of this fluid. Its articulations become easy by practice; repose makes it lazy. There are syllables and letters that it seems hard for it to mark. For example, the initial *s* is reflected there with difficulty. I observed all these things from the first moment when Rodolphe commenced to hear.*

* See Note 25, page 171.

Sound, reflected in the temporal cavity, passes afterward into the vestibule of the labyrinth, and is there divided by reflecting itself anew, in order to be distributed according to its nature. Here is executed the second act of audition. Doubtless it would be difficult to support upon proofs *de facto* a theory so new, but minds that are just and free from prejudices will easily feel its force. Noise is here distinguished from sound; and as I have strong reasons to think, the articulated voice is here distinguished from sound and from noise. Noise passes into one of the ramps of the spiral, and causes those cords of the bony spiral blade that are attuned to it to resound. Sound is insinuated into the opposite ramp, and causes the membranous cords of this same blade that are in harmony with it to vibrate; whereas the articulated voice puts into movement, in the semicircular canals, the unknown notes that are analogous to its articulations. Thus is executed, in different places, the third act of audition, which thenceforth becomes a complete faculty.

This theory explains how my young deaf-mute was able to hear noises without hearing sounds, and to classify the inflections of my voice before

any other resonance. It remains to be known
why, among sounds, the deepest have been the
first to be grasped, and why the vocal articulations
have fluctuated for a long time, and even still
fluctuate in his ear.

I have said that noisy or sonorous bodies produce noises or sounds relative to their inner contexture and to the frequency of their vibrations.
Now the spiral blade which separates the two
ramps of the spiral, and which turns as a screw
around its shaft, is larger in its lower part, and
diminishes in size up to its top; so that the trans-
verse fibres that compose it, whether bony or
membranous, become shorter and shorter like
the strings of a keyboard, and offer relations proportional to and harmonious with all sounds, of
whatever nature they may be, that are accessible
to the ear. But the temporal cavity, the vestibule of the labyrinth, the two ramps of the spiral,
and even the semi-circular canals, are filled with
an air more or less dense, more or less dilated,
more or less sympathetic. If, for example, the
air which serves as echo in the temporal cavity is
denser than that which resounds in the vestibule
or which rules in the two ramps, then the inferior

cords of the bony or membranous blade could be disturbed without the superior ones being at all disturbed. For the air, too rarefied in the higher part of the spiral, would have no *rapport* with the denser air, where the sound would be retained or the echo formed; or if the echo, dulled by long repose, reflected the articulations of the voice feebly, this wavering reflection would wander about without fixing itself in the semi-circular canals or would be fixed quite wrongly. Finally, since there are two ears, if cords of the membranous blade of the one did not accord exactly with those of the other, the individual would always hear badly, and would ordinarily have a false voice; unless, by the effect of steadfast labour on himself, he succeeded in attaining, even as I have myself done, the abstraction of one of his ears to hear only with the other.*

Furthermore, as there are in the spiral blade fibres of different lengths, which can be affected by sounds distinct or simultaneous, it can be admitted, with Euler, that there are also in the air analogous molecules which differ in degree of energy; so that, when two or more sounds, mingled

* See Note 26, page 171.

with diverse noises are brought together to the ear by the same mass of air, they are differentiated by the modified parts of this mass, analogous to each fibre. Thus many different tones sounded near a keyboard make each string which is in their unison resound.

Here, *Monsieur et bon ami,* is the physical theory of the auditory faculty hurriedly explained. You can now unite it to the intellectual theory that I developed in my first letters, and you will have, in its entirety, the system of sensation and understanding of sounds that form the sense of hearing, such as I conceive it according to the experiments that I have made and of which I have related to you a part.

With renewed, etc.

FABRE D'OLIVET.

LETTER IX

Fabre d'Olivet to Ferrier

PARIS, April 25th, 1811.

IT is almost impossible that you should have read my last letter with any attention whatsoever, without having drawn from it an irresistible inference concerning the general cause of deafness. Why should I leave you any longer in uncertainty upon this subject? In supposing even that you may still be uncertain despite all I have said, your perspicacity will find no less the truth therein, although my friendship may have lost the pleasure of having shown it to you. Besides, if these letters are to be made public, I do not wish to suppress anything I can say that may become useful to suffering humanity. Perhaps studious men, of able mind and pure heart, understanding the cause of the malady, will be glad enough to have found its remedy. I earnestly hope that this may be so, I assure you; and I shall neglect nothing, in my other works, to put them on the path of a thing which they can understand, but which must remain hidden to the masses, and above all to the flagitious, because of the wrong use that they might make of it.

Yes, *Monsieur et bon ami*, the general cause of deafness, whether original or accidental, is found in the air which occupies the temporal cavity, called improperly the *ear-drum*, as well as the vestibule of the labyrinth, and the other canals which compose the interior ear. This air, when too dilated in the first cavity, where the echo is formed, renders the sonorous reflection difficult there, and constitutes what is called *hardness of the ear;* when too dense or irregularly compressed in the labyrinth, it causes therein troublesome ringings and insupportable noises; when rarefied to excess in the upper part of the spiral or in the semi-circular canals, it effaces high sounds and the delicate shades of the voice; finally, when wholly absent or lacking in these essential parts of the auditory system, it causes complete deafness therein, for no kind of sound or noise can be propagated in a vacuum.*

In reflecting upon the simplicity of what I have just said, and upon the numerous discoveries that the physicists seem to have made in these same properties of the air from which I deduce the cause of the diversity of audition and of deafness, you will doubtless be astonished that they have not discovered this cause; that they have not indicated it to the medical men, and that these latter have not thereby sought the means of curing deafness.

---

* One feels, according to this theory, that one might perhaps succeed in making certain acoustical instruments, in the interior of which the air would be more or less compressed to facilitate audition. These instruments would be for the ears what telescopes are for the eyes.

But, my good friend, purely physical knowledge does not suffice to arrive at such results. The auditory faculty, however perfect it may be, does not alone constitute the sense of hearing, and it is necessary, as I have told you, to join thereto the intellectual faculties, to transform sensation into sentiment, and unite understanding to audition. It is necessary for every need that speculative intelligence elaborate experimental understanding to perfect knowledge. The fruit is born more slowly than one imagines. It appears to be developed without trouble because the labour that procures it is hidden from the eyes of the vulgar. It is as the voyage of Columbus, the map of which even the commonest sailor soon believed he knew.

In general, the empirical physicists scorn speculative philosophy: and the medical men, drawn on by scholastic dogmatism, receive little outside enlightenment. Nearly all of them incline toward absolute materialism, and believe learning to be contained in positive knowledge. Since Cabanis told them that there was nothing intellectual in man, and that the soul was a faculty of the body, they have believed it on his word, and have limited themselves to physiological studies. Everywhere they see only fibres and blood, only muscles and humours,—in a word, only matter. The spirit, the soul, the morals, are things to which they do not deign to pay the least attention. Many even smile disdainfully when one speaks of them. Not long since they purged and bled largely, as our theatre still reproaches them for doing; today they appear to have turned away from this excess only to fall into another: they cover their patients with blisters and believe to obviate all evils thereby.

I ask their pardon for drawing their attention for a moment to this subject, and for speaking of medicine without being a medical man. But I am a man, and it is by this title that I perhaps have the right to speak to them. Blistering, which they formerly applied only in the last extremity, has the same disadvantages as bleeding when used unseasonably and without a determined need. It is a blind instrument, a sort of medical vampire, which indiscriminately draws the substance from the body, gives to humours a movement that is contrary to nature, and takes away from the patient a force of which he ordinarily has need. Gangrene is often the consequence of its inopportune usage. Not long since I witnessed an event which still makes my heart ache. A young girl of nine or ten years, the idol of her family, was attacked with a comatose fever accompanied by some symptoms of typhus. The doctor who was called in ordered a blister. The evil resisted. He ordered a second, a third. He had a boiling sinapism applied to her feet. Its effect spread over the legs and took the skin off, but the patient did not come out of her stupor. He administered another sinapism. It made no difference. By his orders the head of the young girl was shorn, an epispastic cap was brought. Then I dared to observe to him that this was rather much. He told me that it was the course approved of by the Faculty. However, the father of the young girl called a second and a third doctor. They consulted, they changed their minds, but it was too late. The fever yielded of itself, as it would have yielded without all this display; the typhus symptoms disappeared, and the patient died after frightful pain, devoured by gangrene.

I would awaken your attention, my friend, to the danger of blistering, because I know that since the healing of Rodolphe, many doctors, imagining

that I had healed him by clearing the ear of the
humour that filled it, have enveloped the head
and neck of many deaf-mutes with epispastic
plasters. These means might perhaps, although
with difficulty, succeed in an accidental and incip-
ient deafness, because it is possible that an effusion of humours obstructs the auditory canals.
But it is very poor understanding of nature to
believe that any humour whatsoever could cause
an original and complete deafness, any more than
a cap of iron or a wall would cause it. If the
effused humour can be one of the accessory causes
of absolute deafness, it is when, after having de-
composed the air indispensable for the propaga-
tion of sounds, having absorbed it, or transformed
it into different gases, it changes itself into a sort
of wax, which ends by drying, lining the interior
walls of the cavities and closing up the outlets.
When it has arrived at this condition of hardness,
it is inaccessible to the action of blistering. While
it is still liquid, it can only cause a partial deafness. The real congenital deafness, that which
brings muteness with it, is always the result of the
absolute vacuum of the auditory canals, whether
this vacuum proceed from a natural defect, or

whether it be the consequence of an absorption of the air, caused by local heat, or by a corrosive humour that has hardened after having corrupted it.

These, *Monsieur et bon ami*, are the details that I promised you. May they satisfy your mind as much as I am certain they have interested your friendship! I have said all that I believe can be said. Later, and in works more appropriate, I shall give to studious men the means for succeeding in finding the remedy of the evil, the cause of which I have just explained. Meanwhile, allow me to quote here what a Mandarin of China, writing upon medicine, said nearly a thousand years ago:

"Yes, botany, chemistry, anatomy and medicine have in our days gone beyond all the barriers at which the preceding centuries have seen them arrested. Genius and study have led them into the sanctuary of nature; the torch of experience has shown them its mysteries; the veil that hid from them its most secret sources has fallen. At last these sciences have come to change even poisons into remedies. But does one die sooner or later in the capital and in the great cities, where they display all their resources, than in the country . . . ? O blind men! . . . are you aware that these sciences, and medicine in particular, are only means in the hands of Providence, beneficial when It employs them, and harmful when It does not make use of them? The discoveries and the progress of medicine are a real good without doubt, but only in the case where they augment the forces of Providence to draw us from the dangers wherein we might precipitate ourselves despite It and despite ourselves, and wherein It wishes not to let us perish. . . . Listen to this aphorism of the doctors of old that modern ones no longer understand:

"'Heal often in uniting the action of the remedy with that of the evil; draw from the second the efficacy of the first; abet its malignity to exhaust it; divide it to weaken it; be quick with it to conquer it. Know you the great principle, the great goal toward which you must tend? Behold it: release the plenitude and fill the emptiness.'"

Adieu, *Monsieur et bon ami*. I renew the assurances of my friendship.

FABRE D'OLIVET.

ULTERIOR EXPLANATIONS

(2ND EDITION, 1819)

ULTERIOR EXPLANATIONS

(2ND EDITION, 1819)

THE preceding correspondence was published, and notwithstanding the efforts made by the Imperial Government to stifle it, was known through Europe. I received letters of felicitation from all the countries in which the love of humanity and that of science are not strangers. Indeed certain quodlibets and even certain calumnies were indulged in; there was talk on the subject of the copper casserole, whose magic sound had, it was said, worked a miracle upon the auditive organ of a deaf-mute; but in a century so fecund in able logicians, there was not found a man who dared to raise a logical argument against the veracity and authenticity of the phenomenon. Certain insignificant talk held *sub rosa* in certain salons, came to me, but nothing was published. Such was the condition of things, when the hatred of Napoleon, not content with the reserve I affected, and judging my position still too favourable, laid the snare, an account of which I have given in my Preliminary Explanations. It is known how, notwithstanding the sort of promise I had given not to try other experiments, I had been led to give the auditive faculty to Louis Veillard, a young deaf-mute and former pupil of M. l'abbé Sicard.

I shall not return to the absurd disturbance caused by this event; neither to the *procés*, nor to the persecution which it drew upon me. I have spoken quite at length of it, and the issue is known. But I ask in good faith, of every impartial and dispassionate reader, if it were true that the government of Napoleon, or Napoleon himself, had really wished to know the truth, were there not a thousand means of doing so? Could not one have been informed at Aubonne, at Lausanne, at Geneva, whether the grandson of Major Grivel, who was distinguished and well-known in the canton of Vaud, was really a congenital deaf-mute? Nothing could have been easier than to obtain the proof, since I, a simple individual, deprived of the means Napoleon was able to employ, had obtained it at the very time when I was being persecuted. This fact once well established it would only have

been a question of knowing whether this same
Rodolphe Grivel, who was well known as having
been congenitally deaf and dumb, and who had
remained such despite all the aid from medical
science, now heard and spoke. As there was no
doubt that he neither heard nor spoke, one of two
things must necessarily be: either that nature,
quite alone, had given him the faculty she had at
first refused him, or that she had been aided by
me. One feels clearly that, reduced to terms so
simple, the question should have soon been solved.

But to know the truth was precisely what
Napoleon did not wish.

The truth has always something disagreeable
for tyrants, even when it does not concern them;
with still more reason when it may wound their
pride or provoke their hatred. They always fear
truth as an enemy with whom it is necessary to
entertain the least possible relation. However, so
long as Rodolphe Grivel alone was present in the
arena, Napoleon dared not attack me openly: he
felt himself too weak against such an adversary.
It was not until my too great kindheartedness had
consented to introduce Louis Veillard into the
arena, that he rushed upon me, profitting by this

incident, which he had had the cunning to produce. He triumphed as has been seen; but does not his triumph itself accuse his perfidy?

Now, I ask once more, was it Veillard alone who should have been examined? Was it he whom I had presented to Europe as congenital deaf-mute to whom I had given the auditive faculty? Was it not always Rodolphe who was the important subject and upon whom attention was fastened? Who knew of Veillard? Had I published anything about him? Had I affirmed that the auditive faculty had been given to him? Not at all. I had kept him four or five days at my home so that he might model my portrait. Nevertheless what was done? This act, so simple that on any other occasion it would have passed unnoticed, was taken advantage of; it was turned into a public crime; it was used as a pretext to persecute me; five times I was taken to the *préfecture de police;* a very estimable young woman was summoned there to give reasons for the goodness of heart, the generosity which had influenced her to wish to assist in the healing of a deaf-mute, her compatriot.

The unfortunate Veillard was taken possession

of, convicted, at the age of twenty-one years, of
having taken steps to be cured of a natural deafness without consulting his master, an engraver of
precious stones. He was sequestered from society,
the utmost means were used to make him admit
that I had administered remedies to him; one
wished to know what remedies; whether they were
soft or hard, sweet or bitter. It was noticed
that he smelt of musk; inquiry was made concerning musk; his closets were burst open; it was
discovered that some of his effects were perfumed
with it: great discovery! The heads of three
or four deaf-mutes were covered with linen soaked
in musk; it was thrust into their ears. They were
not healed, consequently my remedy was worth
nothing. The thing is obvious. Finally, the
guilty one, that is to say, Veillard, was made
to appear before the commission which was to
judge him. He was asked questions concerning
the medicine of which he knew nothing; he refused
to reply. Certain noises were made around him
which he did not hear or did hear.* It was stated
that he heard nothing, and a few days later, he
was forced to depart for Geneva.

* See *Documentary Proofs*, No. 3. Page 183.

Is it in this manner that sensible people should act? Louis Veillard had asked permission of the Minister of the Interior* to live with me for a time, in order to develop the auditive faculty he had received, and to share in the lessons I was giving Rodolphe. I myself had offered, touched by the distressing state in which I saw him, to receive him gratuitously. Who, therefore, prevented the Minister from granting so just a request? It was the advice of the *préfet de police*, according to what he himself told me; it would have been the advice of any reasoning man. For, what risk was there in putting me in the position of performing a second phenomenon, under penalty of invalidating the first? Not any. Why, therefore, did not the Minister consent? Certainly one cannot accuse either his perspicacity, or his kindness; for all those who have known M. de Montalivet outside his ministry, will render justice, as I have, to the qualities of his mind and to those of his heart. One must, therefore, see here a more powerful hand, which forced his, and accept the unimpeachable proof of that secret hatred which Napoleon bore me; a hatred which he showed in the first year of

* See page 229. *Tr.*

his Consulate by a decree of proscription from which I might not have escaped, as I have already said, except for a sort of miracle; a savage hatred which I was obliged to elude by a seclusion of twelve years; an irreconcilable hatred in fact, which pursued me everywhere, and which could only be terminated by his downfall or by my death.

I admit that the injustice of the tyrant, of which I knew the causes, was less trying for me than was to him the indifference with which it was received. One would say that, like the head of Medusa, this man had the power of petrifying everyone. With heart frozen into a sort of insensibility, which I noticed also in my contemporaries, I put off making my appeal to posterity, and this would still be unaccomplished if unforseen circumstances had not induced me to follow another course.

The downfall of the imperial colossus, the return of the legitimate Monarch, the upheaval which followed the escape from the island of Elba, and many other circumstances into the details of which it is needless to enter because they are foreign to the subject with which I am occupied, gave me the opportunity of printing my work upon the Hebraic Tongue and the Cosmogony of Moses.

142 The Healing of Rodolphe Grivel

I owed to the generosity of the King,* to his paternal goodness, to the rigorous exactitude with which the government kept its promises, although in a very difficult time, the good fortune of seeing published a book, to the composition of which I had sacrificed the best years of my life. Whatever may be the judgment of posterity, it cannot be denied I think, that it is the result of persevering labour and the fruit of profound meditations. The correction of the proofs of the two volumes in 4° which compose this work occupied me for a full year, from 1815 to 1816, a memorable time, and one which the French will long remember. In concluding this work I had need of a change, and I resolved to employ the time of leisure which followed, in visiting the Cevennes, where I was born, and to embrace my mother whom I had left there twenty-five years before.

It was during this sojourn that I made in my native land, and whilst tenderest memories came to visit me, that I bethought me of a collection of Oscan poetry which I had published in my younger days.† I had long forgotten it. But the sight of

* Louis XVIII, 1814–1824. *Tr.*

† *Le Troubadour, poésies Occitaniques du* XIIIe *siècle,* published in 1803. *Tr.*

those places frequented by the Troubadours, the old chateaux in ruins that I met at every step, those solitary echoes that recalled their songs in repeating the accents of their tongue still spoken by the mountain shepherds, all led me to look this work over again, and plan to make it more generally useful by adding a grammar and a vocabulary. I thought that it would be well to give to the French grammar this support, which it lacks, so as to give the reason for an infinity of things, which, not being derived from the Latin tongue, have remained until now inexplicable; as, for example, the formation of certain compound tenses in the verbs, and the singular anomaly that has been observed in what are called participles. There does not exist today in Europe a single educated grammarian who does not know that the tongue of the Oscan Troubadours, called Langue d'Oc by the natives, was the first modern tongue formed after the extinction of the Latin tongue, and that the first gleams of poetry and of literature that shone forth after the long darkness that followed the irruption of the barbarians, were the work of the Troubadours.

This plan of mine, the execution of which was

thwarted by several obstacles, followed me to Paris. I shared it with several literary friends and with a few savants who approved of it. I composed then the introduction to the work that I planned upon the Langue d'Oc, and published it as prospectus. I received encouragement and many promises for subscriptions. I resolved, in order to give the grammar and vocabulary of the Langue d'Oc, the chief object of my labour, all the perfection of which they were susceptible, to journey again into the Cevennes mountains, and into the adjacent countries where this tongue was best preserved. I acquainted the Minister of the Interior with my design so that he might approve of it and give the necessary recommendation to the *préfet* and local authorities to facilitate my literary researches. This Minister, a friend of letters and himself a distinguished *littérateur*, readily felt the utility of my labour, and had the kindness to enter into my plans, writing me a letter upon this subject as flattering as honourable.

I was, therefore, preparing for this journey, when I received a visit from M. Tromparen, pastor and president of *l'Église consistoriale réformée* of Privas. He was sent to me by the same Peer of

France to whom my gratitude has already done
homage, as being very much interested in the
learned researches upon the Hebraic tongue with
which it was quite well known that I was profoundly
occupied. M. Tromparen, being acquainted with
the object of my journey, offered to be my companion, and urged me strongly to make some stay
at his house in Privas, both in going as well as on
my return, to put my literary materials in order
and to rest myself awhile. I accepted his offer,
which I attributed at the time to his love for
knowledge. But having reached his home, I was
not long in perceiving that he had another motive;
a motive undoubtedly praiseworthy and which it
would be difficult to blame. Nature had afflicted
him with a daughter congenitally deaf and dumb,
and he entertained hopes that I could give hearing
to this child, as I had given it seven years previously to Rodolphe Grivel, whose healing was
known to him. I resisted his appeals for a long
time, still hurt by the persecutions I had endured
under Napoleon's government, and nettled by
the indifference shown me; but finally considering
that that government, as tyrannical as arbitrary,
was no more; that a legitimate Monarch, reigning

at last over France as father of his subjects, would behold only with joy another blessing diffused among his children, I determined to do that which a father and a mother tearfully begged of me.

Between the 12th and the 15th of July, 1818, I developed the auditive faculty in their daughter Nina, four or five years old, whose ear gradually admitted all sounds, from the lowest to the highest, and whose mouth accustomed itself to stammer a few words.

The success of this first experiment having surpassed the expectation of this interesting family, Madame Tromparen proposed a second, arousing my sympathies in behalf of a young girl fourteen years old, and likewise a congenital deaf-mute. This second attempt succeeded still better than the first.

It was the 17th of the same July that I undertook this experiment; a day which I shall never forget, and which doubtless will remain equally engraven in the memory of the reputable persons who witnessed the phenomenon presented to us. The miracle, for I can name it thus, was instantaneous and complete. Never, with whatever expression I might make use of, could I describe the affecting scene that transpired amongst us. Emilie was seated upon Madame Tromparen's lap; I was standing a short distance away, and placed in such a manner that the child could not see me. Hardly had I struck the small drum which I held in my hand than Emilie gave a start; astonishment, pain and joy were depicted at once upon her face. She turned quickly in my direction and looked at me. The expression of her eyes cannot be described; there was something sublime in them. I struck the sonorous instrument anew. She gave more of a start than was manifested the first time. Madame Tromparen, moved to the utmost, feared that the child would fall into a swoon; I stopped; I left the drum and took up the violin. The sound that I drew from the lower strings produced soft sensations upon the auditive organ, and surprise without pain; but as soon as I reached the higher sounds, *la, si, ut, re*, in playing on the third string, the features of the young girl changed, and it was evident to us that she was suffering. I returned to the lower tones of the first two strings, and harmony was established. After several other experiments, being no longer able to doubt that Emilie's ear was entirely opened, Madame Tromparen joined the hands of the child, raised them toward heaven, and made her give thanks to God for a blessing which could only come through His mercy.

In the meantime, M. Tromparen, transported with joy to see his child brought into a new existence, had written to several of his colleagues. M. Maraval, pastor of Aigues-vives, being also afflicted with a child congenitally deaf and dumb, came immediately to Privas, with his wife and his son. I consented to attempt a third test, the success of which was still more favourable. On the 31st of this same month, Adolphe Maraval, nine years of age, received from my hands the auditive faculty.

A few days later I departed from Privas and turned my steps toward the Cevennes, there to engage in my literary occupations. At first I had a fairly quiet life; but, in passing on to Ganges, which is my birthplace, I found that the news of the events that had occurred in Privas had preceded me. M. Tromparen had transmitted the details to my old friend, M. Ferrier.* I was unable to refuse their entreaties and those of several persons

* See *Documentary Proofs*, No. 7. Page 195.

of distinction to see a young man, about twenty-two years old, a congenital deaf-mute; and although I found the subject too old, and afflicted besides with a sort of paralysis, and although I doubted the effect of my endeavours, I gave them nevertheless through regard for the solicitations of my fellow-townsmen. My work was crowned with happiest success; and on the 25th of August, Antoine Besson, put to all kinds of tests, heard distinctly all noises and all sounds.

This being the state of things, and deeming it impossible that such events could remain long unknown, I decided to write to a distinguished and intelligent woman who held one of the principal offices of the *Ministère de l'Interieur*, to beg her to make known confidentially to the Minister what had taken place, and to indicate to me, with her accustomed kindness, the course that I should follow in the future. She replied briefly that if the cures I had performed were such as I announced them, she could only urge me to go on. "Humanity," she wrote, "offers you a noble work, and the publicity of your marvels will unquestionably bring you much honour. You will find a worthy recompense in the very good that you have done, and in the public esteem of which it is my pleasure to anticipate the evidence, in offering you, etc."

In reading this letter I felt the fortunate influence that a kind and paternal government exercises upon all branches of the administration, and I saw clearly that the hatred of Napoleon, henceforth powerless, left me free in my movements.

But who would believe that this hatred had found in fanaticism an auxiliary worthy of it? Undoubtedly nothing was more unexpected. But here is a case of which it can be said that extremes meet.

Military despotism and religious fanaticism, although essentially different in means, are united in principle and in purpose; in both are exclusive dominion, tyranny, intolerance and frenzy. Nevertheless it must be said that public opinion, today loudly proclaimed, leaves little space for their display. It is separated in a manner that gives them no support. Intelligent observers have even been able to remark that military despotism, at the moment of its greatest triumph, and when the noise of its victories stifled on all sides the cries of its victims, found no real friend outside the precincts of its action. Fanaticism, despoiled of its power by the enlightenment of the century, finds fewer partisans as it obtains fewer advantages.

The harm it has been able to do me has been extremely petty. Of the five individuals to whom I have had the good fortune to give, in a few months, the auditive faculty, fanaticism has been able to take away only one from me; the said Marie Rolland, living at Saint-Hippolyte du Gard. This young woman, about thirty years of age, belongs to poor and uneducated parents. I yielded to their importunities and perhaps too thoughtlessly, without sufficiently assuring myself of the means they might have to care for their daughter and to have her taught, once I had developed the auditive faculty in her. It seems that after this development had taken place, they allowed themselves to be surrounded with superstitious terrors, and to be persuaded that they had committed a great sin in seeking to give their child a faculty which God had refused her. It has even been stated to me that it was insinuated to them that the signs of audition she had received and the words she had uttered were the effect of a diabolical spell. They then took all possible means to destroy this spell, and did so much that they stifled a new-born faculty which demanded, in order to develop itself, the most intelligent and the most assiduous care. It is said that despite all efforts, this girl continues to hear. I do not know. What I do know perfectly is, that with such proceeding as covering her head with wet cloths, it is impossible for her to hear much longer. One can read in the *Documentary Proofs* the account of this incident given by an eye-witness, an old man respected for his age, his intelligence and his position as pastor, which office he had held for more than fifty years.

These Explanations are now concluded. I think that I have said enough to place every attentive reader in a position to give judgment. I know that in several biographical works, the authors, in speaking of me, have had the kindness to say that the legal suit started on the occasion of the cure of Rodolphe Grivel remained suspended. Here is something with which to furnish the decision. I have spoken frankly and truthfully. I am serene.

End of Ulterior Explanations

NOTES ON THE CORRESPONDENCE
(2ND EDITION, 1819)

NOTES ON THE CORRESPONDENCE

(2ND EDITION, 1819)

(1) In terminating my *Preliminary Explanations*, I said that the letter which I wrote to M. Ferrier, an old friend of the father of Rodolphe Grivel, having been almost entirely included in the course of these Explanations, was suppressed in order to avoid useless repetitions. It is replaced here by the reply which he made to it, and which gave occasion for the letters following. Ganges, where M. Ferrier resides, is a small town at the foot of the Cevennes mountains, seven leagues from Montpellier. It was my birthplace.

(2) This letter, which I wrote in a moment of exaltation, is certainly too strong and departs from epistolary conventionality. I would not publish it today were it not already known; but the harm is done. The estimable person to whom I addressed it pardoned the sentiment that dictated it. Her intelligent and sensitive mind

pictured the difficult position in which I found myself and she was not vexed with me for having of necessity dissimulated the situation; but it is not thus with everybody. There are persons who would have wept and augmented the mistakes. The mistakes were obvious, without doubt, but were they worth the bitter sarcasms and the diatribes that were printed in the journals on this subject? I do not think so.

(3) I have suppressed in this second edition a complimentary phrase which I addressed to Napoleon to quiet him. All of this letter sufficiently elucidates what I said in my *Preliminary Explanations*, that I promised him implicitly to draw advantage only from the purely scientific part of the phenomenon performed upon Rodolphe Grivel, and that I pledged myself not to attempt others.

(4) What I say here to Madame B—— R—— concerning the interest with which her children inspired me is true. Never have I experienced so keen a desire to try the felicitous means which Providence put into my hands, as on this occasion. But it was impossible. If at least one of the children of this lady did not receive the auditive

faculty from my hands, she must accuse not me, but Napoleon, who would not allow it. I was so moved with good-will toward her that, notwithstanding the peril to which I exposed myself, I indicated to her, in terminating my letter, an indirect means of doing what she desired. She did not perceive it, or rather I believe she was prevented from perceiving it, its nature being perverted in her eyes. It is useless to mention it in this edition.

(5) It is now, at the moment of writing these notes, nearly five years since I have heard from Rodolphe Grivel, who is living at present in Aubonne, his birthplace. But according to the reports that several persons have made to me, persons who have recently spoken with him, it appears that my observation was correct. He has, in his speech, preserved a very strong accent, quite similar to that of a Swiss who would speak French with difficulty. I think that this is owing partly to his age at the time when he received the auditive faculty, and partly to his strongly pronounced organic constitution. I have reason to believe that Nina Tromparen and Adolphe Maraval, who received the faculty at a much younger

age, and who are endowed with more delicate and mobile constitutions, will not experience the same inconvenience.

(6) This system, that I show here on a small scale, circumscribed in one sole sense, I have developed on a large scale, applying it to all metaphysical man, in my examinations of the *Vers Dorés de Pythagore*.

(7) This was exaggerated, in my opinion, in consequence of the unfortunate experiment which was made upon Rodolphe. He was stunned by a noise too loud, as I shall tell further on, and ran the risk of losing all through a lack of understanding, quite excusable however in a situation so novel.

(8) This theory is explained too briefly here; it is indeed given in principle; but the developments are lacking. It is necessary to read what I have indicated above in the examinations of the *Vers Dorés*.

(9) I give the name of *means* to the thing which, known in the ancient sanctuaries and quite clearly announced in the first chapters of the Sepher, can facilitate the passing of life into an organ which is deprived of it. The word *reméde* is found

in the first edition of this work; but this word was badly chosen.

(10) Here is the unfortunate copper casserole which has given rise to so many quodlibets. One was right in making it a subject of censure, for one could find nothing worse; but was the raillery well in its place? Oh how insensate men are! How envy and the desire to injure one another injure them themselves. How prompt they are to propagate error, and how stupidity finds the credulous for them! One would say that it is only toward truth that they are slow and suspicious. How are those writers who are not madmen and who make public profession of respecting their readers able to explain that I pretended to heal deaf-mutes by striking upon a casserole? How have they found men disposed to believe them, men who have not crushed under foot a lie so fatuous, so deficient in all that goes to make a calumny piquant? One must be indeed dull of wit, even in the absurd where it abounds, not to find anything better against a man whom the secret hatred of a tyrant leaves defenseless to the darts of his enemies.

But let us pass over their foolishness and let

us see in what they are right. It is not because a casserole carries with it a commonplace and ridiculous idea that it should not have been used on this occasion; but because it makes, when struck forcibly, a loud sound capable of giving paroxysms to a deaf person whose ear admits a noise for the first time. He risks having the auditive faculty wrested from him forever, by the breaking of the organ which is its seat. Rodolphe fainted in being its victim; and as the experiment has taught me, I do not doubt that the extraordinary empty spaces which are encountered in his ear, as for example, the impossibility of admitting *fa sharp* and *sol sharp*, when it admits *fa natural* and *sol natural*, were the result of this disastrous test.

Loud harsh sounds, all those which make the interior cords of the organ vibrate violently, should be carefully avoided. The same mistake was made with Rodolphe as one would commit with a blind person for whom one had just removed a cataract, if one suddenly flashed upon his eyes the glare of a burning brazier or a lighted torch. The first sounds that a deaf-mute should be made to hear ought to be low and soft; those of a small drum are the best in this case and they are those which I used afterward with Nina Tromparen, Emilie Pourret, Adolphe Maraval, etc.

(11) Rodolphe could do this, because he already knew the written language, and because he could understand the meaning of what I made him articulate; otherwise it would have been impossible, for it would have been inconsistent.   No being, whatever his intelligence may be, can be ignorant of and know a thing at the same time.   Therefore, expecting a deaf-mute to comprehend the moment he can hear and speak, is expecting him to understand and not to understand what he does: which offers a flat contradiction and consequently an impossibility.

(12) This, however, can be modified according to the character of the individual and the circumstances in which he finds himself.   I have seen only children of a tender age experience anything like this.

Nina Tromparen, about five years of age, after the first impression and the first joy, paid no attention to the new faculty which she had received.   This faculty was developed in her almost unconsciously, as with a new born child.

Adolphe Maraval, nearly nine years old, found himself fatigued after the second trial, to the point of wanting to escape like a headstrong child to whom one gives a bitter beverage to swallow. But after one or two scenes of caprice and rebellion, he became calm and gradually accustomed himself to receiving the impression of noise.

Emilie Pourret, thirteen or fourteen years old, at first gave marks of admirable sensitiveness; but after the first days she became sad, as had Rodolphe Grivel, and fell into a sort of melancholy. She sought out lonely places and often it was observed that she hid her tears. It seemed that even after six months of hearing she was not wholly accustomed to it; and I am told that although she has made quite evident progress in the exercise of speaking, her amazement still continues as well as her melancholy.

Antoine Besson was twenty-two years old when he heard for the first time. He had fervently wished for this grace from heaven and his joy was therefore very keen. Nevertheless, he was unable to escape entirely from the influence that noise exercised upon his awakened organs. A certain stupor followed his first joy. And this stupor, which somewhat resembles a great bodily fatigue, returns from time to time, particularly when the air is humid and the weather rainy.

Marie Rolland, thirty years of age, unable to resist the fatigue of hearing noise, after having wished for the auditive faculty with extreme eagerness, has sought to annihilate it with equal impetuosity. It is true that fanaticism has entered into her transports by the terrors and superstitions with which it has surrounded her. Certain gossips of the town, as unacquainted with charity as with the enlightenment of their century, have taken advantage of the piety of this young woman and her inclination for ascetic ideas, to convince her that the fatigue which she experienced was a just punishment from God, who having made her deaf and dumb, would not wish her to acquire a sense He had refused her.

(13) I have been led to make the same observations regarding Emilie Pourret. I questioned her after a storm and she gave me the same explanations as Rodolphe had given me. Her parents believed that she heard the thunder, but she admitted that she only felt it.

(14) All this has been the same with all the individuals.

(15) In the *Preliminary Explanations* I have told the consequences of this pious but thoughtless procedure.

(16) Rodolphe Grivel already knew the French tongue through writing, such as had been taught him at the *Institution des Sourds-Muets*, and this knowledge made it much easier for him. None of the deaf-mutes to whom I have since given audition had this knowledge; also their progress has been from the first much less rapid. Will they not be more sure in time? Time will tell.

(17) I have seen these things repeated in the same manner. Emilie Pourret, slightly melancholy as I have said, liked very much to sit alone by the side of a pond, and while within range of observation was seen to strike the water gently with a stick or stir it with her hand and incline her ear to hear the murmur. Nina Tromparen, who has a brother younger than she, would take him aside and repeat the articulated sounds which she heard him speak. When she was in good humour she uttered all sorts of sounds, accompanying them with very expressive gestures and facial

movements to imitate the conversations she heard but did not understand. Antoine Besson at first imagined that all the sounds he heard had a meaning, and that one could understand what the birds said. One day while walking with his father and passing over the gravel, he heard the crunching of the stones beneath his feet; he believed they were complaining at being thus crushed, and wanted someone to explain to him what they said. Being at his window, several days after his ears had been opened, a merchant of boxwood combs happened to pass, who cried out in the vernacular of the country: "Penches de bouy! Penches de bouy!" This phrase appeared to him so pleasing that he instantly retained it and was delighted to repeat it, amusing himself therewith for a long time. I recall, as one of the most extraordinary things of this nature which has come to my attention, that Louis Veillard having gone to walk in the Luxembourg, at Paris, with M. Servier, two or three days after he had been presented to me by Mlle. R———., stopped in front of a statue of Bacchus, and pointing his finger at it, said, with an effort of intelligence almost inconceivable: "Hey, Bacchus!"

(18) This idea could be the subject of very curious experiments; but I have not had the opportunity to make them.

(19) In general, I have found deaf-mutes sensitive to music as soon as the ears have been able to receive its sounds; but of all the ears I have examined thus far, I have not found any better organized than those of Marie Rolland, who has since taken an aversion for that faculty which she had so much desired. I have seen this young woman, and a great number of persons have also seen her, distinguish among the three lower strings of a violin, *sol, re, la,* the one that had been played at a certain distance behind her. I have seen her, two or three days after her ears had been made capable of receiving sounds, listen to those of a tambourine, a violin, and a flute, compare them and depict by her gestures the different instruments without making a mistake. The persons who were present at the first experiment, to which she lent herself very gracefully,* can remember that while she was absorbed in repeating the three or four words that she already comprehended, *pain, vin,*

---

* I shall name among these persons, M. Durand, *pasteur du Culte réformé,* M. Boissière, *docteur en médecine,* and M. Sabatier, *ancien militaire, commissaire de police de la ville de* St. Hippolyte du Gard.

eau, a street-singer stopped on the square near the place in which we were, at a distance of about one hundred or one hundred and fifty paces, and there began to sing, accompanying himself with a tambourine; the young woman, acutely moved by the sounds of this instrument, seemed to start up suddenly as from sleep, and indicating to us with her hand the direction whence they proceeded, made us understand the kind of instrument by placing the right forefinger in the palm of the left hand, and tapping upon it as she would have done upon a real instrument.

(20) Emilie Pourret at Privas furnished me with a much stronger proof of this same fact. I have said that this young person was endowed with great sensitiveness. One day after having bandaged her eyes we placed her by herself on a chair with a stick in her hand while we ranged ourselves in a half circle in front of her. I made her understand that she was to listen well, and that after she had heard one of our voices, to direct her stick toward the one whom she believed had pronounced the word *papa,* which she was accustomed to hearing us pronounce. She occupied herself with this exercise for some time; and we observed that

as the word *papa* would strike her ears, she usually directed her stick correctly toward the place from which the sounds came, especially when the voice was low and strong. Several times she made mistakes; but her mistakes themselves, at which she heard us laugh, and at which she herself laughed in pulling away the bandage, served to verify her attention and the value of the experiment.

(21) All the experiments I have made have confirmed these several facts.

(22) All the deaf-mutes who have succeeded in acquiring the auditive faculty are as decided as Rodolphe upon this point. Never have I made them hear sharp sounds of the flageolet without their having experienced a visible uneasiness, and the greater their nervous temperament the more irritable they appeared. The first time I made Nina hear this instrument she flew into a rage against me; and the first time Emilie heard the sound, she wept with pain. Adolphe Maraval escaped from us and ran away at full speed. Marie Rolland, although passionately fond of music, experienced a convulsive shuddering. Besson alone endured it without moving a muscle.

But it must be known that this young man, besides natural deafness and dumbness, was also affected with a nervous condition which made him almost stupid. This condition, which seemed to tend toward paralysis disappeared with the deafness.

(23) I recall that the servant of M. Tromparen, seeing us make the daily experiments upon Nina's ears, wished also to experiment and without our knowledge. One day therefore, she placed herself behind the child, and at an unexpected moment whistled very loudly. It seems that this whistling was disagreeable to Nina and *roughed* (to use Rodolphe's expression) her ears violently; for she turned around quickly and gave the servant, who was greatly astonished to see she had heard so well and whose face was within reach, a hard slap.

(24) Everything tends to prove this truth. My theory of the sense of hearing, such as I have deduced it from facts, and as I have explained it in my VII and VIII letters, is found constantly confirmed by experiment. I have already said that in a *Mémoire* received from Milan an account was given me of an accidental deafness, which manifested itself by loss of the highest sounds and

finished by loss of the lowest ones. This course, inverse in the acquisition of these same sounds, has been confirmed for me since by another *Mémoire* coming from Switzerland. From still another quarter, a professor of Marburg, Germany, named M. Markledeg, wrote to me upon the same subject and assured me that he still heard many noises without being able to grasp the sound of any word addressed to him. I have myself seen, at different times, many persons who are deaf through accident, whose deafness has begun likewise with loss of sharp sounds and the high inflections of the voice.

Whilst I was occupied with classifying my first observations, in 1811, a son was born to me. Two learned physicians who saw him when less than two months old, MM. Albert and Marie de Saint-Ursin, considered him extremely advanced both in strength and in intelligence. From the time of the birth of this child, and during several days following, I made different experiments upon his auditive organ; and I was convinced that inharmonious noises were the first admitted. After noises, the inflections of the voice excited the auditive sensation, and very low sounds did not begin to affect it until after noises had done so. At the age of six weeks a clapping of the hands or the fall of a heavy object made him start, whereas the higher sounds drawn from the flageolet caused him no emotion. At the age of three months I saw him turn his head at the sound of a voice, and still remain unmoved at the higher notes of an instrument. He obviously heard the noise of a drum, whereas the sound of a violin or a flute did not seem to cause him any sensation. Thus the development of hearing in Rodolphe at the age of fifteen years did not differ from that I observed in my son at the age of fifteen days. In both the development of hearing took place from low to high and proceeded from the inharmonic to the harmonic.

(25) I have noticed these same things in all the subjects whom I have had within reach of observation. The hissing of the *s* has always been the last articulation admitted into the ear of deaf-mutes.

(26) It must also be considered that there exist some individuals with whom the ramps of the spiral and the semi-circular canals adjacent contain certain imperfections. It may happen that

some cords in the membranous labyrinth are lacking and that those tones corresponding to the articulations of the voice may be absent or obstructed in one of the canals. In the former case, one sees that the ear, accessible to certain sounds, refuses to admit certain others; and that, in the latter case, it remains absolutely insensible to certain vocal inflections. This very important observation explains the notable dissimilarities that different peoples produce in their musical scale and in the number or the nuance of their articulations. One knows, for example, that the Orientals who follow the musical system of the Arabs, and who take the tone *re* for the fundamental tone, instead of the *ut* which we take, give to *fa natural*, which is the third natural of this same *re*, a quarter of a tone more than ours; so that their natural *re* tone is neither *major* nor *minor* exactly, according to our manner of speaking. This *half-sharp fa* sound, thus constituted, which is pleasing to their ears, is intolerable to ours; which shows a difference of organization, and certainly depends upon the natural cause that I indicate. One also knows that the Arabs, and all the peoples sprung from the same source, are unable to articulate the consonant P, which they assuredly could do if their ears were not insensible to its nature; for this labial consonant is not difficult. The Chinese nation, which consists of more than two hundred millions of individuals, has remained insensible to the articulations of the consonants B, R and Z; and among the American tribes have been found many whose speech lacks more than half of our vocal articulations.

End of Notes.

DOCUMENTARY PROOFS

(2ND EDITION, 1819)

DOCUMENTARY PROOFS

(2ND EDITION, 1819)

No. 1

ACTE DE VÉRITÉ, *delivered by the entire family of Rodolphe Grivel, and written out by the grandmother, Madame Grivel, in form of a letter to her daughter-in-law.*

I thought, my dear daughter, that an account given by your father, together with the certificate of the authorities, would be necessary for you to convince those who doubt the healing of your dear son, and who pretend that he has never been either deaf or dumb. I did not believe that doubt was possible, after having seen him treated as a deafmute at the institute; the thousands of witnesses here who knew him from his birth, will support our testimony, if it should be necessary. The truth told quite simply, may, perhaps, convince the unbelievers, and we shall find ourselves very fortunate if it contributes to your peace of mind and to that of our friend, and proves to him, though poorly, our gratitude and our acknowledgment.

Your son, born very robust, had none of those diseases common to children and was treated accordingly. The extreme attachment of his parents caused him to be often in their arms. When he was about three months old, I perceived that he was insensible to the noises made to distract him from crying, whether by rapping upon the windows, or by shaking a rattle within his reach. I spoke of it several times to your mother, who, wishing to banish a distressing truth, denied it, or gave worthless reasons for it. He did not even try to lisp. Having attained the age when children know their parents, and especially the mother who nourishes them, he fondled you with caresses analogous to his faculties, but which every day strengthened my fears. At last when he was three years old, your husband consulted M. Prelaz, the town physician, who was very well known for his splendid cures in medicine and in surgery, and who, after having examined the child frequently and given him some remedies, decided that he was deaf and consequently dumb. With surprising intelligence he learned, we know not how, to pronounce certain monosyllabic words, common to all deaf-mutes; but with his comrades he used only gestures to make himself understood, and they were never misinterpreted. Before the death of his father you took him to Geneva, where M. Turène examined his ears in a room arranged for such purposes; and he confirmed the decision of M. Prelaz. This grievous affirmation caused your husband, already very ill with consumption, to think of the institute of abbé Sicard. It was upon his dying bed that he exacted the promise that you send your son there. He died soon after, very much concerned with this project. Wishing to avoid the expense which Rodolphe's sojourn in Paris necessitated, you took him to Geneva. M. Monoir, a well-known surgeon, cared for him a long while; he made two cauteries behind his ears; galvanized him for several months; but no relief from the affliction was obtained for this dear child. After a third examination by these *Messieurs*, to whom were added, through friendship for the family, MM. Durant and Colladon, physicians, they decided the child was deaf and dumb. Rodolphe, not being quite old enough to be received at the institute, was taken to Aubonne, where his grandmother taught him to write the alphabet; but all his lessons were done by gestures and signs. A few years later he was confined to the tender and sympathetic cares of M. Colladon, who took him to Paris, and the following day to abbé Sicard. All Paris has seen him in the public and private exercises, treated as a deaf-mute. In order to be nearer to your child, you renounced all the comforts of a private life and accepted the position which you now occupy with Madame Servier.

Here, my dear daughter, is the concise summary of the infancy of our dear child, and the signatures of the relatives who were with him constantly, and who saw him daily until his departure. I embrace you both tenderly.

AUBONNE, January 7th, 1812.

Signed in the original: R. Grivel, *major, grand-père;* Jeanne Grivel, *née* Valier, *grandmère;* B. Grivel, *grandoncle;* Louise Grivel, *tante;* Prelaz, *médecin;* Henriette Valier, *cousine affectionée;* F. Secretan, *pasteur;* Allié Grivel, *cousin;* Valier Grivel, *juge d'appel;* Muret Grivel, *inspecteur des milices du canton de* Vaud; Marianne Grivel, *cousine;* Charlotte Valier, *cousine;* Charles Valier,

cousin et ami; Louis Grivel, *ancien sous-préfet;*
Charlotte Vionnet, *cousine-germaine;* Pauline Vionnet, *cousine-germaine.*

I, the undersigned, Susanne Vionnet, *veuve*
Grivel, mother of Rodolphe Grivel, do certify that
the above writing, signed by M. R. Grivel, *mon
beau-père,* contains the most exact truth. At
Paris, January 25th, 1812.

Signed in the original: S. Grivel; T. S. Grivel;
Berier, of Lausanne, *lieutenant du préfet* of the
canton of Vaud, and member of the *grand conseil;*
C. Bergier; S. Bergier; Jean Pierre Colladon.

I knew Rodolphe Grivel upon his arrival at abbé
Sicard's; he was deaf and dumb.

Ravel Dangirard.

NOTE. It was after the date of the *acte de vérité*
which has just been read, signed by all the members
of a reputable family, of which many have been or
still are in the most important civil and military offices
of the canton of Vaud, that they dared to print and
publish before the eyes of Europe that Rodolphe Grivel
was not a congenital deaf-mute, and that he had heard
and spoken until the age of four years. To such a
degree did Napoleon exercise a powerful influence and
know how to make light of what men hold most sacred!
For confirmation of this *acte,* see the following numbers,
4, 5, 6.

No. 2

Extract from Rodolphe Grivel's journal.

Saturday, March 9th, 1811.

M. Sicard, my kind director and my kind guardian, M. L——, my doctor at the institution, came to the door of my room, and rapped; I said to them: *Enter*. They came in with Mama. I embraced affectionately M. Sicard, whom I asked, speaking the words, how he was? He replied to me that he was very well. We went together to M. Fabre's who spoke to them for the first time of my healing. . . .

M. Sicard wrote to M. Fabre, to tell him that Friday, March 15th he would come again. He came at noon to M. Fabre's, who came into my room to call me, so as to see M. Sicard. I heard what M. Fabre and M. Sicard dictated to me. They talked much with pleasure. M. Fabre told him of the journal of my thoughts, he was pleased with it and he laughed at it. . . . M. Sicard wanted to embrace M. Fabre because he admired him.*

* It is necessary to remember, in this number and in the one following, that they are in the style of two deaf-mutes; and one should look for neither purity nor correctness of grammar.

No. 3

Extract from the correspondence of L. Veillard.

L. Veillard, to his *maître d'apprentissage*.

October 19th, 1811.

My very dear master, I announce to you that I have been healed of deafness by M. Fabre d'Olivet, with God's aid. . . . I thank the good God infinitely, as well as M. Fabre d'Olivet. I thank you for letting me go with Mlle. R——. I want to tell you that I am very gradually hearing the noises of carriages, of glass, of the drum, etc. M. Fabre d'Olivet spoke loudly and I heard a little. He opened the window of this room and I heard it well. . . . While I was awake at fifteen minutes after four on Saturday morning, I heard someone knock three times. The same day I faintly heard someone blowing his nose. M. Fabre d'Olivet has taught me to speak a little. I said: *I like you.* . . . He heard me well. I want to tell you that I am constantly modelling on the portrait. . . . Adieu, with heartfelt love and most respectful greeting.

Report of L. Veillard to the *Préfet de Police.*

November 4th, 1811.

I want to tell you that I learned with surprise
and wonder that M. Fabre d'Olivet had healed the
deafness of Rodolphe Grivel. I went to Mme.
Servier in order to examine Grivel and to talk with
him. The same day I tried knocking softly with
one of my fingers upon the pane of glass in his
room. In fact, he quickly turned around toward
me, and he heard it very well. I was convinced
of it. I got ready to write to M. Fabre d'Olivet;
that is to say, I asked him to agree to heal me of
deafness. He replied to me. After he wrote me,
I did not go to M. Fabre d'Olivet's. He decided
to ask *mademoiselle*, his friend, to beg M. J—— to
permit me to go with her to the country. But
I was mistaken. She took me to her home. She
told me she was a friend of M. Fabre d'Olivet.
She told me that I should go with M. Servier to
his home so that M. Fabre d'Olivet might heal me.
I did not know him. But I was astonished and
overjoyed to stay with M. Fabre d'Olivet to be
healed of deafness. This was to be a pleasant
surprise for M. J——. In fact, I was healed by
M. Fabre d'Olivet.

After that you may think I heard directly and all of a sudden. I must say no. But I heard a little, gradually, the noises of the wagons, of the violin, the piano, glass, the drum, etc. I heard a little when one spoke loudly. I heard a little when one blew his nose, or sneezed, or coughed. *Papa, mama, tata,* etc. . . .

I arrived at M. J——'s the next day. The next morning my comrade asked me to go to his room to help him lift his table. He knocked it with his brush. I heard it well although I was quite far from the table. He was even more astonished than I was. I am satisfied to hear little by little. Be sure of that.

I modelled in red wax the portrait of M. Fabre d'Olivet. When he wanted to pay me 36 francs I refused it.

I greet you with deep respect.

L. Veillard to M. Fabre d'Olivet.

November 23rd, 1811.

. . . I have been out from here twice, for my errands. I have heard well the noises of carriages, and especially of carts. I was in our court-yard;

I heard someone knocking. I turned quickly around, but I saw no one. I asked . . . if someone knocked. . . . The knocking continued, more and more. I heard it with fear, surprise and joy. I thought someone had knocked very loudly with a big hammer upon the table behind me; but I did not see anyone. I searched about. I asked . . . if someone had been knocking loudly. I was told that a soldier had been beating his drum outside in the street.

To the same.

December 2nd, 1811.

My dear best friend, I want to tell you that two members of the *Institut*, doctors, and MM. S——, J——, T——, C——, and myself were in the *salle d'administrateurs des Sourds-muets* last Thursday. They read for a very long time; they laughed several times. I showed them my report. J—— said to them that I was sometimes a liar. They read several papers for a long time. One of the members of the *Institut* questioned me by writing . . . about the medicine. I did not want to tell them about it . . . M. J—— said *a* three times behind me. I did not hear it clearly, for my sense of hearing was foggy. . . . I asked him to play upon the violin or the piano. . . . He did not do it. He pretended to ring; I told him that I did not hear it, but that I would hear it in time. . . . I told him that when you spoke loudly *papa, mama, oui, non,* I heard a little. When Madame, your wife, spoke *papa* loudly; I did not hear it. . . . J—— raised the blackboard. . . . He struck it with his key. I did not hear it clearly. My sense of hearing was foggy, although I was surprised at the last to have heard twice very plainly. They finished. They left the room.

M. J—— told my comrades that I heard nothing under the eyes of the commissioners. I was surprised at this. . . . I told him angrily that I had heard twice very plainly. . . . He said that M. T—— knocked eight times very loudly with a key upon the blackboard and that I had not heard it; but he struck the ninth and I heard it. . . . I know very well that M. T—— struck it lightly eight times, but the ninth he struck loudly. In fact, I heard it very strongly.

I want to tell you that the two members of the *Institut* were deceived.

No. 4

Acte de notoriété publique concerning the natural
deafness of Rodolphe Grivel.

We the undersigned, inhabitants of the city of
Geneva or its environs, do certify it to be our
knowledge, and known publicly, that the young
Rodolphe Grivel, born at Aubonne, in the canton
of Vaud, the 15th of May, 1796, was a congenital
deaf-mute, having never heard or spoken. In
testimony whereof, signed at Geneva the 10th of
January, 1812.

Signed in the original: P. J. Bridel; Bridel,
oncle; Henri de Mestral; Théodore Cerrise; E.
Sayons; Binet-Marc; L. D. Mesinez; Mallet-du-
Pan; T. Conrad Vogel; T. Massip; J-André Lesage;
G. Cramer; Florentine Lesage, *née* Andrillat; Pes-
chier-Melly; G. Berguer; *veuve* Counis; *veuve*
Brunel; Jenny Binet; Gab. Gallot; Aug. de Maffey;
Susanne Dombre, *née* Brey; P. Saussac; Renée
Saussac, *née* Chastain; J. A. Perisse; A. Blanc;
Isaac Bourdillon; G. Rapingon; Fred. Amiel;
Marie Amiel; J. P. Coutan; J. J. Dudley; F.
Mallet-du-Pan; Henriette Bridel; Ch. Dessieux;
J. Delamorte; F. Lond; Alexandrine Vignier; Jenny

Vignier; Ch. Chatillon; T. Dunant; Dunant, *née* Moillet; Fanni Chatillon.

No. 5

Actes legaux concerning the natural deafness of Rodolphe Grivel.

We, *Syndic, Adjoints et Conseil municipal* of Aubonne, district of Aubonne, canton of Vaud, Switzerland, declare, to the requisition of citizen Rodolphe Grivel, townsman of said Aubonne, former major in the service of the country, that he is the chief *notoriété publique*, that his grandson Rodolphe Louis Grivel, born May 15th, 1796, son of the late Charles Louis Grivel, *conseiller* of Aubonne when living, and of *dame* Jeanne Susanne Vionnet, his wife, came into the world deaf and dumb, it being the knowledge of the council that the said Rodolphe Louis Grivel was treated at Aubonne as well as elsewhere by divers doctors, with the hope of healing him of his infirmities, and that all the sacrifices of the parents of this interesting child and the attentions of the profession to attain this end, were without success, which determined them to send him to Paris, to the *Institut des Sourds-muets*, there to receive the instruction that is given to children afflicted with these two infirmities.

In testimony whereof, issued at the *municipalité*, at Aubonne, under seal of the *Conseil municipal*, the signature of its *président* and that of its *secrétaire* taken the 29th of December, 1811. Signed in the original: Cusin, *syndic;* Doué, *greffier municipal.*

The above-named major Grivel, townsman of the commune of Saint-Livre, presenting himself at the *municipalité*, requesting that an *act de vérité* be accorded him upon the unhappy state of deaf and dumbness of his grandson, Rodolphe Louis Grivel, this *municipalité* has made the same declaration as that here above accorded by the *municipalité* of Aubonne, and this from the knowledge that it has always had of the state of this young man, deprived from his birth of the two above-mentioned senses, until the time when he went to the *Institut des Sourds-muets* at Paris.

Issued with the signature of the *syndic*, with that of the *greffier* of the said Saint-Livre, December 23d, 1811.

Signed in the original: J. Tripod, *syndic;* G. L. Guignet, *greffier.*

Le juge de paix of the assembly of Aubonne, of the canton of Vaud, Switzerland, declares genuine the municipal seal of the said Aubonne, and the signatures of the citizens Cusin, *syndic,* and Doué, *greffier de la municipalité* of the said Aubonne, as well as those of the citizens Tripod, *syndic,* and Guignet, *greffier municipal* of the *commune* de Saint-Livre, assembly of the said Aubonne, elsewhere affixed.

AUBONNE, December 28th, 1811.

Signed in the original: Menthonnex, *juge de paix.*

The undersigned, *secrétaire en chef du petit conseil* of the canton of Vaud, certifies as genuine the above signature and seal.

LAUSANNE, December 30th, 1811.
Signed: Boitol.

Le ministre plénipotentiaire de France, in Switzerland, certifies as genuine the above seal and signature.

Berne, January 2d, 1812, *pour le Ministre, le secrétaire de légation.* F. Rouyer.

Le ministre des relations extérieures certifies as genuine the above signature of M. Rouyer.

PARIS, February 8th, 1812.

By authorisation of the *Ministre*, the chief of the division of consulates, signed: d'Hermand.

By the *ministre*, the chief of the *bureau des passeports*, signed: Brulé *jeune*.

NOTE. Here certainly is the natural deafness and dumbness of Rodolphe Grivel verified as authentically as is physically and morally possible. This child was, therefore, a congenital deaf-mute. The false material put forth by the government of Napoleon is refuted the very moment it is printed; for it must be observed that the *actes*, dated the end of December, 1811, and the beginning of January, 1812, are not subsequent to the downfall of the tyrant. They are, on the contrary, signed at the moment of his greatest power.

No. 6

Extract from a letter of M. Corver Hooft, at the time *Chambellan de l'Empereur*, to M. le colonel Gordon.

Monsieur,

You ask, in the letter with which you have honoured me, if I can give you some information concerning M. Fabre, and concerning the almost

miraculous cure of young Grivel, which he performed, and upon the authenticity of which I
learn with amazement that doubts have been
raised. Although personally unacquainted with
M. Fabre, I find myself in a better position than
anybody else to satisfy you in this regard through
the relations that have existed for a great many
years between my family and that of the young
deaf-mute for whom M. Fabre undertook and performed the cure. The mother-in-law of Madame
Grivel lived for sixteen years in our family pre-
siding over the education of all my sisters, whom
she left only when they had no further need of
her tutelage. It was not until after her return
to Switzerland that the young deaf-mute was born.
His birth, as the only male branch of the family,
and afterward his infirmity, which was soon manifested, were the subjects of a great many letters
in the correspondence that she has always maintained with my family; so that I have never lost
sight of this young man. Moreover, I have never
failed to go to see him each time I have been in
Paris since he was placed in the *Institut des Sourds-
muets*, and each time I have heard the best testi-
monies concerning his intelligence; but I never

remarked that anyone had raised the slightest doubts as to his deafness. It was not until last February, having gone to visit him, as was my custom, that I learned that his mother . . . had taken him away from M. Sicard . . . to try to give him the faculty of hearing. . . . I went straightway to Madame Grivel's, where I found her son, in nearly the same state as before; and no one speaking to me of the cure, I thought no more about it until I was informed by public reports, and finally by a letter from his grandmother, who was herself reluctant to believe in the miracle. I was at that time in Holland; but, upon my return to Paris I was a witness to the truth of what I had heard. During six weeks I visited him several times, and I observed marked progress as much with reference to the faculty of distinguishing sounds as to that of articulating them. M. Fabre, whom I had never seen and who had made the acquaintance of Madame Grivel only by chance, has had the kindness, knowing the interest I take in this young man, to enter into the greatest details with me, not alone respecting the cure, but also respecting the motives that induced him to keep it secret until its success should prove its efficacy; and I have found them dictated by prudence. . . . Believing to have satisfied, *Monsieur*, the questions you had in mind in addressing yourself to me I have the honour of being, etc.

Signed in the original: J. Corver Hooft.

Amsterdam, March 23rd, 1811.

NOTE. I could add here many similar letters; but besides uselessly enlarging this collection, they could add nothing to the validity of the assertion of a man whose reputation for honour and probity is so strongly established as that of M. Corver Hooft.

No. 7

Proofs relative to Nina Tromparen
Extract from a letter of M. Broussonnet, *doyen* of the *Faculté de médecine* of Montpellier, to M. Tromparen.

MONTPELLIER, May 1st, 1818.

Monsieur,

It is very painful for me to be forced to repeat to you that the malady of your daughter offers no other chance of relief than that which might be procured by an event of which there exists no example. One has seen the faculty of speech reestablished suddenly; but the words the individuals have uttered prove that they have learned them by the aid of the sense of hearing, which seems to be destroyed with your child. It probably was so destroyed in a convulsion during infancy; only an instant suffices to consummate the evil.

Therefore I do not advise any kind of treatment, which would only tend to impair the health the little girl enjoys and which although continued over many years, would not lesson her infirmity; you would act more wisely by beginning at once her special education so as to make up the deficiency of the two senses which she will lack.

I repeat all the regrets that I feel in having only consolation to offer you, etc. . . .

Signed: D. Broussonnet.

NOTE. I possess a similar letter from Dr. Chrétien; but as it is only a question here of establishing the natural deafness of Nina Tromparen, that of a savant as commendable as M. Broussonnet is more than sufficient.

Extract of a letter written by M. Tromparen, father of Nina, to M. Ferrier, of Ganges.

PRIVAS, August 4th, 1818.

Without having the honour of being known to you in any way, you have rendered me a most

important service: some time since, you vouch-
safed to beg your worthy friend, M. d'Olivet, to
attempt the healing of my deaf and dumb daughter.
Your generous solicitation had great weight with
him; and contributed not a little to the great deed
he has accomplished and to the happy event that
has followed it. M. d'Olivet will himself relate
all to you. I am confining myself to informing
you that he left yesterday for Saint-Hippolyte,
after having sojourned here for several days, which
he devoted to my child. The attempt was crowned
with most propitious success. The ear has been
rendered susceptible to sounds. This is proved
as clearly as her age, under five years, can permit. A thousand proofs have demonstrated the
fact. It remains for her to distinguish sounds,
the most difficult thing imaginable, and to articulate certain monosyllables. She is on the road;
I have the calmest as well as the happiest conviction of it. While my wife and I are occupying
ourselves with this cheerful labour, our thoughts
will often be carried to the revered friend of our
greatest benefactor.

M. d'Olivet has not limited his inexhaustible
goodness to my child. Two other cures have been

attempted, and while having no better success, they have been more striking because the subjects upon whom they were performed have themselves made it clearly understood that hearing was given them. One is a girl of fourteen years who begins to articulate monosyllables; the other is the son of my colleague, M. Maraval, pastor at Aigues-vives, who having brought here his son, nine years of age, has had the good fortune of taking him away endowed with the precious sense which nature, by a whim too frequent, had refused him.

Excuse, *Monsieur*, the liberty that I have taken to entertain you with these wonderful events, and deign, etc.

Signed: Tromparen, *pasteur*.

NOTE. I possess many letters of M. Tromparen, which contain details of the progress made by Nina and Emilie since the time of their cure; I have made extracts of the most marked facts and have reported them in the preceding notes. Repetitions would be superfluous.

No. 8

Proofs relative to Adolphe Maraval
Actes concerning the natural deafness of this child.

We, the undersigned, *pasteurs de l'Église chréti-enne réformée consistoriale* of Montpellier, department of Hérault, do certify and attest to whom it may concern that Célestin-Adolphe about seven years of age, son of Jean Maraval, *pasteur de l'Église consistoriale* of Aigues-vives, and of Anne Paux, is in a state of absolute congenital muteness, and that he has neither heard nor spoken to this day. In testimony whereof, etc.

Done at Montpellier, July 28th, 1817.

Signed in the original: A. Lardat, *pasteur* at Pignan; A. L. Lissignol; H. Michel, *pasteur* and *président du Consistoire*.

I, the undersigned, *médecin du Collége royal* of Montpellier, do certify to having been consulted, about four years ago, in regard to the child above named, by which I am convinced, by all the proofs proper to establish my opinion, that he was veritably suffering from the infirmities of which mention is made.

Montpellier, July 29th, 1817.

Signed: Chrétien, *médecin*.

I, the undersigned, *docteur en médecine* and *professeur de pathologie* in the *Faculté de médecine* of Montpellier, do certify that it is to my knowledge that young Célestin-Adolphe Maraval, son of Jean Maraval, *pasteur de l'Église consistoriale* of Aigues-vives, is a congenital deaf-mute, and that he is keenly desirous that some method be applied to him for the reintegration of this double animal function.

Montpellier, July 27th, 1817.

Signed: Baumes.

Extract from a letter of M. Maraval, father of Adolphe.

AIGUES-VIVES, September 5th, 1818.

Monsieur and most esteemed friend! . . . My child, as you have foreseen, has not been stationary. You recall the state in which you left him; since then he counts upon his fingers the hours of the clock, and one day his mother saw plainly that he heard it striking without his attention having been called to it. He has distinguished very well a number of sounds: the braying of a donkey, the crowing of a cock, the beating of a drum at quite a distance, etc., etc. He pronounces the R, the V and the F. He pronounces CA, by putting one of his fingers between his teeth. He says *tata* very well; after several attempts he succeeded, the 31st of last month, in saying *mama*, which caused Madame Maraval a pleasure for which she had longed and which she believed to be still very distant, . . . a pleasure which one can indeed imagine, but not describe. Since then Adolphe has always called my wife by the tender name of *mama*, even as he has called me by that of *papa*. Finally I have made him understand that he is called Adolphe, and when I make him hear this name at a short distance, he turns and replies to me, *papa*. Often he goes to lie down in a corner and calls, sometimes to me, sometimes to my wife, to know if we can hear him. . . . I have already received tidings from my estimable colleague M. Tromparen; he informs me that his little girl begins to give them satisfaction; that she now pronounces seven or eight monosyllables and that she would pronounce a greater number of them if she were not hampered by the exertion of making the sounds. He also told me that Emilie continues to make progress in respect to speech; that her voice is softening; and that, as to her hearing, she constantly makes it understood that she is enjoying it. . . . Accept, etc.

Signed: MARAVAL, *pasteur*.

NOTE. The further correspondence of M. Maraval contains details of his son's progress. He informs me, in his letter of October 3rd, that the vocabulary of this child is considerably enlarged. He tells me that he has been unable to prevent several persons, distinguished for their learning from Paris even to Montaubon, from becoming acquainted with this phenomenon.

No. 9

Proofs relative to Antoine Besson.

Acte de notoriété publique concerning the natural deafness of this young man.

We, the undersigned, inhabitants of the town of Ganges, department of Hérault, do certify that it is known publicly and to our intimate knowledge that the said Antoine Besson, son of Antoine Besson and of Marie Delpusch, born in the above-said town of Ganges, the 23rd of January, 1795, has been constantly known and reputed to be afflicted with natural deafness and complete dumbness, never having given any obvious sign of audition, or uttered any kind of articulate speech before the 25th of August of the present year. In testimony whereof, etc.

Signed in the original: Ferrier, *fils*, *négociant;* Ferrier, *père*, *propriétaire foncier;* Deshons, *propriétaire foncier;* De Darvieu, *juge de paix;* Matthieu Randon, *fils;* Beziès, *fils;* M. Randon, *négociant;* Randon *père*, *avocat;* E. Rous, *négociant;* Dupuy *et* Rolland, *négociants;* Bourdon, Ducros-Figarel, *ancien maire;* Jean Lafont, *ex-premier suppléant du juge de paix;* Gervais, *chef de bataillon;* Pierre Cazalet, *négociants;* Conduzorgues, *notaire;* Gounelle, *propriétaire foncier;* G. Soulier Tarteron, *ex-directeur des domaines;* Mourgue-Dalgue, *négociant;* le *maréchal de camp* Soulier; M. Durand, *ancien pasteur de* Ganges; D. Francezon, *négociant;* J. F. Lebre, *négociant;* Isaac Tarteiron, *ancien juge de paix;* C. Gaussorgues-Tarteiron; Ausset, *négociant;* J. Pascal, *neveu;* J. Lafont, *propriétaire foncier;* Caizergues, *propriétaire foncier.*

Seen for the authentication of signatures, Ganges, November 11th, 1818.

Signed: AIGOIN, *maire.*

Seen for the authentication of the signature Aigoin, *maire*, Montpellier, November 27th, 1818.

Le Préfet de l'Hérault

CREUZÉ DE LESSER.

204 The Healing of Rodolphe Grivel

Extract from a letter of M. Besson *père*.

GANGES, August 30th, 1818.

My dear *monsieur*, I took my son to the Temple.
When we entered, he began to smile, hearing
M. Detienne read; perceiving that he heard, he
was transported with joy. The people who were
nearby noticed it. The child makes progress.
When he salutes people he says to them, *good
day*. The people are astonished to hear this. I
have many other things to tell you of the child's
progress. The spelling-book that you left, he
knows it by heart. . . . I close in offering pray-
ers to God for you and your family, etc.

Signed: BESSON.

NOTE. M. Besson being obliged to work at his trade
of making stockings was unable to give his son the
necessary care; but M. Lafont, a lawyer, former as-
sistant of the justice of the peace, was willing, through
benevolence alone, to charge himself with this difficult
labour. He has instructed this young man very zeal-
ously, and has caused him to make more rapid progress
than another might have done. His last letter informed
me that Antoine already pronounces a great number of
words, and replies to many questions.

No. 10

Proofs relative to Marie Rolland.
Copy of a letter written by M. Durand, *ancien pasteur* of Ganges, resident of Monoblet, near Saint-Hippolyte.

To the Editors of the *Archives du Christianisme*.

A man of profound thought, who in himself represents many men, has been attracted to these regions by motives foreign to the subject of which I am about to speak. This unusual man is M. Fabre d'Olivet. During a journey which he made into the department of Ardèche for geological and literary researches, a M. T——, of Privas begged him to stay a few days with him to put in order his materials; and M. T—— profitted by this occasion to present to him one of his children, a girl of five years of age, congenital deafmute. M. Fabre d'Olivet examined her; in two days she heard and a few days later she spoke.

This first astonishing success was followed by a second in the neighbourhood. The rumour of these two events was spread as far as Gard. The father of a family in Aigues-vives, in the environs of Nismes, having heard of it, had recourse to the same means for his son, five years of age, who was afflicted with the same infirmity as the other children. He obtained the same results. This child, cared for by an intelligent father, already begins to speak with facility.

These different facts were announced to me by men whose testimony I cannot suspect; but they were not eye-witnesses. Considering this I said to myself: the exaggeration delighted in by lovers of miracles would give to these diverse deeds a consistency which seen at close proximity would disappear. Without believing anything I did not deny anything; I was neutral, and I awaited the moment when I might have more light in which to fix my ideas. This moment arrived.

At Ganges, three leagues distant from my present domicile, a town in which I lived for several years, and which I left a short time since, there is a young man, nineteen or twenty years old, whom I knew in a personal way, who was likewise a congenital deaf-mute. M. Fabre d'Olivet, earnestly solicited by the father of this youth, saw him, and the following morning, in a public meeting, he gave unequivocal signs of audition. These details were transmitted to me by judicious, incredulous persons who were present at the gathering. For once I had nothing to reply; I was vanquished, but not convinced. It must needs be that I see; and the time was not long delayed.

At Saint-Hippolyte, which is a short league from the place where I am living, a young woman, thirty years of age, was treated for the same infirmity. I learned accidentally that she would show herself to the public at her home, and I set out at once to present myself. This young woman appeared radiant, with a calm, angelic joy; her soul seemed to have left its wonted abode and settled upon her countenance. A flute and a violin were played at a reasonable distance behind her. As the instruments rendered delicate sounds which touched lightly the organism of her ears, sounds soft and languishing which gently stirred her sensibility, a quiet smile showed itself upon her lips; and she indicated with her forefinger, by imitative gestures around her ear, the softness and slowness of the sounds which struck it. While we were absorbed in watching what was happening, a vendor of songs, descending from the street which cut at right angle the street on which we were, stopped at the corner, in front of an inn at a distance of about a hundred paces from us, and played on a tambourine. Soon the young woman gave a start; and although the windows of the room were closed, and although she absolutely could not see the player, she indicated with her hand the street whence the sound came, and imitated the movements of the musician. A glass of water, some bread, some wine and several other objects were shown her, and she was asked what they were called. To every one of them she applied the proper word.

I am omitting several other incidents because those I have mentioned seem sufficient.

All of the facts that I have just related are common knowledge and could, if necessary, be vested with judiciary forms. At Ganges particularly, the entire town would rise up, if need be, to attest that the young man of whom I have spoken, a congenital deaf-mute until the 24th of last August, heard and spoke on the 25th, the same day as the *fête du Roi*. A rare tribute! and very worthy of the paternal Monarch whom Providence, after tempests too prolonged, has replaced upon the throne of his ancestors.

But let us consider the sequel of the treatment
of the young woman from Saint-Hippolyte. While
the others in whom the sense of hearing was developed advance rapidly in the course of speaking,
this one has been arrested at the first steps. She
is poor and has been put to the rough work of the
field; she is without instruction and has been surrounded with fear. Fanaticism, child of ignorance, has said to her parents, and they have made
her understand, with that tone of inspiration
which persuades weak and simple souls, that it
is a horrible sin to try to give oneself a natural faculty that God Himself has refused; that one must
remain such as one was when leaving the hands of
the Creator; and that the effects produced upon her
were by diabolical spells. Credulous and timid,
she became possessed with terror; she refused the
help offered her; enveloped her head with wet
cloths, exposed herself to the inclemency of the
weather, so as to revert to her primitive state of
deafness; it appears that she has indeed relapsed
into that state. Should it not be thus with frivolous discoveries that might be favourably wel-
comed? But all those which bear the august
imprint of truth, of usefulness, should they be

opposed and rejected? In the sciences, Galileo
was persecuted for having taught that the earth
turned on its axis. Descartes was obliged to
take refuge in Sweden for having founded scholas-
ticism. In the arts, the intervention of tribunals
was necessary to establish the usage of quinine
and emetic. Every influence of the government
was needed to spread the use of inoculation and
vaccination; and today one seeks by all manner
of means to stifle a discovery which essentially
concerns humanity.

When will this calamitous strife finish? It will
only finish when the prejudices that support it are
extirpated. These prejudices are so active that
they attach themselves to politics, to religion, to
nature, to society, to customs, to private relations, to everything; and they torment men in the
name of a merciful God. These are the sparks
which sometimes produce conflagrations in States.
Let the writers in their works, the men charged
with public instructions whether civil or religious,
and the men vested with a great moral strength
unite together to combat and to destroy the
hundred-headed hydra of fanaticism! Fanaticism
is the box of Pandora which contains all evils

and scatters them over the earth; the man who destroys it will be the benefactor of humanity and he will attain social immortality.

M. DURAND, *pastor.*

APPENDIX

APPENDIX

The following Letter to M. Ferrier is relative to the progress of the healing of Rodolphe Grivel. It was originally included in the text of Fabre d'Olivet's own handwritten script now in the possession of *La Bibliothèque de la Société de l'Histoire du Protestantisme français* and was copied by the Translator through the courtesy of Monsieur Weiss, *secrétaire.*

Fabre d'Olivet to Ferrier

PARIS, August 25th, 1811.

It is exactly four months ago today since I wrote my last letter to you about young Grivel. I know, *Monsieur et bon ami,* that you are impatient to know the sequence of the extraordinary event of which this son of your old friend has been the subject. But I have wished, before writing you again, to let things proceed, and to give myself time to examine them quietly. They have at last reached a decisive point and I take up my pen again to inform you of them.

Rodolphe entered a private institution on the fifteenth of this month. Seven months of exercises and lessons have put this deaf-mute in condition to hear all noises and all sounds of the voice, to grasp them and classify them, to express by speech all his thoughts, to make understood all his needs, and to comprehend through a slowly articulated language, everything that is not outside the sphere of his own ideas. I have now judged it proper to turn him over in a measure to himself. To accustom him to hear other voices than mine, I have placed him with strangers, in the midst of twenty young boys to whom he is wholly unknown. In order to avoid the bad results that the knowledge of his past infirmity might bring about, and above all to prevent the use of the sign language from which he detaches himself with difficulty, and toward which his natural timidity and habit of fifteen years of dumbness draw him despite himself, I have exacted of the master of the boarding-school that his former condition be known to himself alone and that Rodolphe pass in his school as a young for-

eigner, a Polander, come to Paris to learn the
French tongue, which he still speaks very badly
and which he understands with difficulty. All is
arranged according to this plan. Rodolphe, lodged
in a private room, under the surveillance of this
instructor, four times a week receives lessons from
a professor of French, whom his mother has
chosen, and lessons from a music master. He goes
to classes for writing and arithmetic as an ordinary scholar; and twice a week he is brought here
for me to judge of the progress of his pronunciation
and his comprehension, and to give me the opportunity to continue the acoustical experiments of
which his healing has been the aim and the means.

These experiments are of too great importance
and pertain too closely to the reasons that made
me undertake the extraordinary cure, in which I
have had the pleasure of succeeding, for me ever
to leave their direction to others. I have done all
I could to render these experiments profitable to
general and particular science, I have not evaded
any visit and have not closed my door to any
person, honest and well known, who was curious
to examine the results. Without inviting the
savants individually, I have seized every occasion

to give evidence of the satisfaction I should have
in receiving them. Unfortunately (I do not know
whether it be to their shame or to mine), I have
been very little disturbed.

When certain thick clouds, which ignorance and
bad faith have jointly raised and sustained, shall be
brought down by their own weight to the mire
that has produced them; when Truth, freed from
these envious vapours, shall shine with all its
éclat, astonished posterity will ask how it is possible that in a city like Paris, where the love of
science seemed carried to such a high degree of
exaltation, where nothing seemed to cost too much
in the exploration of the works of nature, where
reigned twenty opposed systems upon the crystal-
lization of fossils and the organization of vege-
tables, where discussions raised upon the origin
of speech and the formation of ideas had brought
forth thousands of baseless reasonings, a human
being dumb and deaf from the instant of his
birth, had obtained, after fifteen years of dumbness, the use of hearing and of speech, without
one of these savants, who were so curious to measure the angles of a mineral and to follow the flight
of a butterfly, deigning, during six months, to

take a step to inquire into the prodigy! I only fear that posterity, for which there will no longer exist that common phrase with which the lazy and the ignorant content themselves today, *that is not true*, may not take from the actual science and the love it inspires, an idea proportional to merit.

Concerning the persons who have written or spoken publicly on the healing of Rodolphe, three alone have done so with knowledge of the case: the pastor to whom the mother of this young man confided the care of presenting his thanksgiving to God; M. Lombard, a student; and M. Marie de St.-Ursin, a doctor of medicine. The others have not seen him and consequently have only been able to write or speak blindly and according to their prejudices or their interest. I shall be careful not to call attention to their blunders or show the weakness of their reasonings; this would draw them from their tomb, and give them a life of which they are not worthy. I shall only say, to show the source whence the sharpest darts come, that in a country where Pascal and Fréret, the strongest dialectitions of the modern world, have traced the laws of dialectics, it is only the sophism of baldness that has been found to oppose me. Now, my good friend, do you know what this sophism is? I am about to inform you and to show it to those who have used it perhaps without knowing it. I said in my *Preliminary Notice*, at the head of these letters I have written you, that the only words young Grivel could pronounce at the age of nine years were those common to all deaf-mutes, those which result from the joint action of the labial consonants, *mama, papa, bobo.* Thereupon a powerful logician, armed with the brain of Eubulides thrust upon me an argument that amounts to this: what is a bald-headed man?

"What is a bald-headed man?"

"One who has no hair."

"But, if this man had one hair would he still be bald in your opinion?"

"Yes."

"And if he had two?"

"Even the same."

"And if he had three, four, five, six. . . ."

It is evident that in exhausting the series of the numerical units, the man in question would come to a point where I should be forced to admit that he was no longer bald.

"Then," my subtle reasoner would continue,

"one single hair is sufficient to prove that a man is not bald, and three prove it more; and since you agree that your mute uttered three words at nine years of age, I maintain that he was not mute; for I prove that a word constitutes speech, in the same way that one sheep is sufficient to form a flock and one single grain of corn to give the exact measure of a bushel."

Very good. But if this must go on so, whence comes it that Buffon so improperly calls deaf and dumb a young man, who, by his admission, could pronounce not only three words, but thirteen hundred, by which he acknowledges that he also has intelligence? Would it not be because the words pronounced are nothing to the sense of hearing, upon which speech uniquely depends? Because, without hearing, veritable speech cannot exist, though one pronounce by mechanism all the words of the tongue, as the heads fabricated by Vaucanson pronounced them. Now if ten months of time was sufficient for Rodrigue Pereire to teach the young deaf-mute, of whom Buffon speaks, the thirteen hundred words in question, it seems to me that without having the same talent, assiduous and zealous parents could indeed teach their child to articulate, by imitation, three or four of the easiest words such as those uttered by Rodolphe at the end of nine years of attention and efforts of all sorts.

I am really ashamed to dwell upon such stupid nonsense, and to be obliged to state, when the works of Buffon and Condillac are in the hands of all the world, that speech could never exist without hearing, nor abstract and general ideas without speech; that speech does not reside in words uttered by mechanism or by imitation, and that a mute does not cease to be a mute by articulating three or three thousand words, any more than a head of wood or a parrot becomes an intelligent being for having articulated certain intelligent phrases.

However, I must not neglect to tell you, *Monsieur et bon ami*, that my theory upon the sense of hearing, as I have explained it to you particularly in my VII and VIII letters, is happily confirmed by experiment. I have told you that in a *Mémoire* received from Milan, I was given an account of an accidental deafness which manifested itself by the loss of the highest sounds, and finished by the loss of the lowest. The inverse progress of the acquisition of these same sounds has been confirmed for me by another *Mémoire* which has come from Switzerland. A professor from Marburg, Germany, M. Markaldeg, has written to me upon the same subject. He asserts that while still hearing many noises he is unable to grasp the sound of any words that are addressed to him. I have myself personally seen several people, accidentally deaf, whose deafness has likewise begun by loss of the shrill sounds and the highest inflections of the voice.

While I was occupied with classifying these various observations, a son was born to me. Two learned doctors who saw him when he was less than two months old, MM. Albert and Marie de St.-Ursin, judged him extremely advanced as to strength and intelligence. From the day of the birth of this child, and during several days following, I made different experiments upon his auditory organ, and I am convinced that inharmonic noises were the first ones admitted. After noises, the inflections of the voice excited the auditory sensation; and very low sounds began to produce this sensation only a long time after noises. At the age of six weeks, a clapping of the hands or the fall of a heavy object made him start; while

the shrillest sounds from the flageolet caused him
no emotion. Now, when he approaches the age
of three months, while he turns his head at the
sound of the voice, he still remains wholly insensible to the higher sounds of an instrument. He
apparently hears the noise of the drum, whereas
the sound of the violin or the flute does not yet
exist for him.

The development of hearing with Rodolphe at
the age of fifteen years has not differed from that
which I have noticed with my son at the age of
fifteen days. Both have advanced from low to
high and have proceeded from inharmonic to harmonic. At the moment I am writing you this
letter, Rodolphe, tested by the violin, has followed
its sound as far as *mi*, which gives the octave by
shifting up the treble-string. When *fa sharp*
above is given, he hears nothing. The interval
of a tone is still for him the measure of infinity.

Adieu, *Monsieur et bon ami*, I shall give the
sequel to this letter when events or facts worthy
of your curiosity shall urge me to write again.
Until then approve of my silence, and impute it
only to the multiplicity of my occupations.

FABRE D'OLIVET.

This letter was furnished the Translator by Monsieur Weiss, secretary of *La Bibliothèque de la Société du l'Histoire du Protestantisme français.*

Fabre l'Olivet to HIS EXCELLENCY *le Ministre de l'Intérieur*

Monseigneur,

I have herewith the honour of addressing to your Excellency a petition sent to me by Louis Veillard, congenital deaf-mute; pupil at first of M. Sicard and now serving as apprentice, at the expense of the government, to M. Jeuffroy, engraver of fine stones. I owe to your Excellency some explanations on the subject of this petition and the request therein expressed.

The healing of Rodolphe Grivel, congenital deaf-mute, which I had the good fortune to achieve, excited the enthusiasm of Louis Veillard who knew his original state of deafness and dumbness. This young man wrote me on the 25th of last August a letter, of which I here enclose a copy,

begging me to render him the same service I had
rendered his old comrade. In the dependent state
in which he found himself, this was difficult, for
I knew without possibility of doubt that his master entertained the most unfavourable prejudices
against me and that he had denied the healing of
Rodolphe Grivel without giving himself the trouble
to see him or to examine him in any way. I expressed my regrets to Madame Servier who, as
compatriot of this young man, was particularly
interested. At that time she told me nothing of
the project she had in mind; but several days later
I knew that a step her husband had taken in this
matter with M. Jeuffroy having been fruitless, she
had greatly interested in favour of this deaf-mute
a lady from Geneva. This lady is a distinguished
pupil of M. Isabey the painter, and was able under
this relation to approach the engraver and ask
for young Veillard to model a portrait. Veillard's
master having consented, in consideration of the
price of 36 francs to be given to his pupil, Veillard
was conducted to Madame Servier's, where I
examined him on Wednesday, October 16th. On
Thursday the 17th I knew that he was curable and
the following day (the 18th), his ears being opened,

the auditive faculty was recalled and manifested its presence in such a manner as to leave no doubt concerning his early healing.

Such was the condition into which I had brought him in four days, when the same lady who had requested him from his master for this space of time, went to announce to him this unexpected healing. She anticipated a transport of joy and thanks for the happy stratagem which had produced so great a good. But her surprise was great when, instead of this, she beheld an access of fury. She found herself exposed to a torrent of insults and was menaced with being sent to the police. At first she thought that only anger and offended egotism inspired a vengeance so unreasonable. She was mistaken. M. Jeuffroy, a few days later, carried out this absurd project, and actually caused to be summoned to the police not only this lady, who was irreproachable in her conduct, but myself, whom he did not know in any fashion and from whom he had never received any kind of injury.

As your Excellency undoubtedly has before you the circumstantiated report of this singular affair, I shall not enter into any details. I shall limit myself to explaining that Louis Veillard has been put into forced seclusion by his *maître d'apprentissage*, surrounded with terrors of all sorts, threatened with imprisonment if he does not reveal my means of healing or if he does not renounce saying that he is healed, and can with difficulty remain in such a state. Despite the surveillance exercised over him, he has found a means of informing me of his condition and has transmitted to me, with a letter for his father, the petition he addresses to you, *Monseigneur*.

Deign to glance through it; and if your Excellency consents to grant its object, I beg you to be so good as to assign for him, not my home, where I positively cannot receive him, but that of M. Salomon, *maître de pension*, *rue Férou*, near St. Sulpice, where Rodolphe Grivel has been living for three months. The society of this former deaf-mute could be very useful to him in the beginning of a new education. I shall gladly consent to give him the lessons necessary for the acquisition of speech, but I absolutely do not wish to receive, either on his part or on that of the government, any kind of remuneration.

I have the honour of being, with sincere respect,

Monseigneur, Your Excellency's very humble and very obedient servant.

(signed) FABRE D'OLIVET.

P. S.   I here enclose a note that Louis Veillard sent me for *M. le préfet de police;* it belongs to your Excellency to whom this affair has returned and in whose hand it should have been kept.

To HIS EXCELLENCY *Monseigneur le comte de* MONTAL-IVET, *ministre de l'Intérieur,* Louis Veillard, congenital deaf-mute, former pupil of M. Sicard, living now with M. Jeuffroy, *graveur sur pierres fines et membre de l'Institut de France.*

Monseigneur,

I have the honour of asking for the protection of your Excellency in a circumstance upon which my welfare depends.

M. Fabre d'Olivet has succeeded in healing my deafness, but a year at least is still necessary to finish his estimable work.   For this purpose it is necessary that I be near him during this short space of time, and as the government pays its pension to M. Jeuffroy, my master of engraving, I dare pray your Excellency to deign to allow me to live with M. Fabre d'Olivet, only for a year, and to grant me at his home the pension which is accorded me at M. Jeuffroy's. When my hearing is restored, I will return to M. Jeuffroy as formerly, and the first words that come from the mouth of an unfortunate being, ill-favoured by nature, will be to thank, after God, your Excellency for so great a favour.

Monseigneur

Your very humble and very obedient servant,

(signed) Louis Veillard.

graveur en pierres fines.

The following letters appeared in *La Gazette de France*, Sunday, March 3rd, 1811. *Tr.*

To the Editors of *la Gazette de France:*

Messieurs, the special attention you give to propagating enlightenment induces me to beg you to insert in your journal a fact which should hold the attention of all, and open a vast field for reflection to those who are seeking to discover to what point the ancients extended the sphere of human achievements. The 3rd of last February, while attending the public worship of the Protestants at the church of St. Louis, I heard, at the close of the service, a very raucous voice pronouncing distinctly enough to be heard by persons farther away than I, the following words, which were dictated to the one who pronounced them: *I thank God for having given me hearing and speech.*

The singularity of the occurrence having excited my curiosity, I asked for information from persons who were interested in the healed young man, whom I had often seen attending the service and being questioned at the public entertainments of M. Sicard. I learned that M. Fabre d'Olivet, known for his profound learning in the Oriental traditions and particularly in the study of the hierographics of Moses, upon the cosmogony of which I was told he had been working for a long time, had healed young Rodolphe Grivel, a congenital deaf-mute, by using means entirely unknown to modern savants and physicians but perfectly known to the ancients.

An occasion to verify for myself a fact so surprising was at last presented yesterday. M. Fabre d'Olivet had the kindness to satisfy my curiosity fully by giving me the most authentic information concerning the deafness of young Grivel; he made him write and speak in my presence; I observed him with the keenest interest; I witnessed the emotion the various sounds caused him; I heard him questioned upon things which could not have been planned.

This young man, fifteen years old, was born at Aubonne, Switzerland, of parents of good position and of honest fortune, who some months after his birth, recognized with sorrow that their child was really deaf. During the nine years of his childhood they did not cease to administer all the curative means that science could furnish; MM. Gay and Prélaz of Aubonne, Jurien, Maunoir and Butini of Geneva, all gave him their care and tried all remedies. Never was a deaf-mute treated with less success; all was useless. His parents having lost all hope, sent him then to the *Institut des Sourds-Muets*, where he remained six years, receiving the education which is given there to such unfortunate beings. M. Sicard discovered signs of genius in this child, took a liking to him, showed him a particular kindness, and was pleased to make him appear in his public entertainments as one of his best pupils. He made him articulate by purely mechanical means, certain sounds which the youth did not understand and to which he could not attach any idea. The Emperor rewarded his progress by according him, in 1807, a place as pupil in the *Institut des Sourds-Muets* at the expense of the government. The mother of this young man, wishing to be near the son upon whom all her affection rested, accepted a place as *sous-maîtresse* in the boarding-school of Mme. Servier, with whom Mme. Fabre d'Olivet was associated.

M. Fabre d'Olivet, having occasion to see young
Grivel and testing his natural sagacity and his
tenderness for his mother, became attached to him,
felt that he would become a more than ordinary
man if the obstacles that were opposing themselves to the development of his faculties were overcome, and believed that his efforts would be
crowned with success if he revived the means
which, in very remote times, were used in the
sanctuaries of Egypt. He communicated his plan
to Mme. Grivel who, having given her consent,
was present, on the 7th of January at the first
experiment. On the 9th the faculty of hearing
was developed, and it was known by unequivocal
signs that the child heard. On the 11th his tongue
began to be loosened, and finally he consecrated his
first words, on the 3rd of February, to thanking God.

Let one imagine a young man entering a new
world, not distinguishing at first the noise of
sound, imagining that all the objects which produce sound are endowed with speech, not com-
prehending any more of his own language, when
it is spoken, than a child of Paris would comprehend Chinese or Persian, and learning little by
little to relate the sounds to certain types, to

classify them methodically, and to attach ideas to
them. Then one might conceive how interesting
his education would be, and be hopeful for new
ideas on the metaphysics of understanding.

We know of blind persons who have recovered
sight, and who have realized by experience our
conjectures upon distance, upon colours and the
shadows which trace the form of objects for us;
but their ideas were shaped, and they had only
to recognize the optical illusions that touch could
rectify as soon as they were formed. Whereas this
young man, being forced to reason constantly in
order to place himself on our level, makes us
hope for knowledge of the liaison of signs and
sounds with ideas; of the assistance they lend
to reflection, of the extension they give to the
faculties of the mind, and of many other problems of metaphysics upon which we can only
conjecture.

I would like, *Messieurs*, to be able to relate to
you some of the observations M. Fabre d'Olivet
has already made while teaching his astonishing
disciple, being persuaded that they would interest the reader; but this would involve me beyond
the limits of a notice that you perhaps will find

already too long; therefore I stop here, hoping that you will kindly inform the public of a fact so interesting under all conditions.

I have the honour of being, etc.,

LOMBARD *fils*, *étudiant*.

PARIS, March 1st, 1811.

The foregoing letter was likewise inserted in *le Journal de Paris*, March 8th, 1811, with some different readings. It was addressed *Aux auteurs du Journal de Paris*, March 1st, 1811. *Tr.*

La Gazette de France

Friday, March 15th, 1811.

TO THE EDITORS OF *la Gazette de France:*

Messieurs, the letter that M. Lombard has addressed to you relative to the healing of young Rodolphe Grivel, congenital deaf-mute, and which you have published, has imposed upon me the obligation of entering into certain details on this subject, for I deem it necessary that a man whose conduct becomes public, in whatsoever manner, should give account to the public of this same conduct. Therefore I have considered that the first thing for me to do in this circumstance, and

remain faithful to my principle, is to make known
the motives that determined me in this act and
the purpose I had in view, reserving the right to
speak later of its result.

It is to fulfill the first aim that I pray you to
give space in your journal to the enclosed copy
of a letter I wrote to a lady, mother of two congenital deaf-mute children, who urged me with all
the effusion of maternal tenderness to attempt for
them that which I had done for Rodolphe. As this
letter is the expression of the truth, I can add nothing more or better to it.

Accept, *Messieurs*, my sincere greetings.

FABRE D'OLIVET, *homme de lettres,*
pensionnaire du Ministère de la Guerre.

The letter to Madame Bazin-Robert, which was
here inclosed, is contained in the text, page 70. *Tr.*

La Gazette de France

Sunday, March 24th, 1811.

TO THE EDITORS OF *la Gazette de France:*

Messieurs, I beg you to have the kindness to
give space in your paper to the letter herewith
enclosed, which I am writing to M. Fabre d'Olivet

to disclaim most emphatically the article in a journal under date of the 16th of this month, which attributes to me an expression of thought that is not mine.

Accept, *Messieurs*, the assurance of my consideration,

F. ROBERT, *née* BAZIN.

To M. FABRE D'OLIVET

March 23rd, 1811.

Monsieur, after having read in *la Gazette de France* the article in which an account was given of the cure you performed upon young Grivel, deaf-mute, I hastened to write you and implore the same favour for my unfortunate children; you did me the honour of replying; and in giving you permission to print the reply you deigned to make me, I begged you not to join mine to it, however affecting the motive might be which had dictated it.

The misfortune of my daughter and of my son makes me feel deeply for all the unfortunates afflicted with the same infirmity, while the interest you yourself take in young Grivel obtains for you the right to my gratitude. The healing of this young man does not appear doubtful to you; but even though success should not crown your efforts, I owe you, none the less, gratitude for having dared to attempt a work so difficult and so extra-ordinary.

Therefore be convinced *Monsieur*, that I am wholly stranger to the article which the editor of a journal allowed to be inserted in one of his numbers; the tone which prevails in the replies that have been attributed to me is not mine and those who know me will not be deceived by it. I know the full extent of the duties imposed upon my sex; modesty is one of the virtues that is exacted of women; it would ill become them to seek to emerge from the obscurity which nature, ever wise, seems to have prescribed. In assuming that great talents (which are not my portion) should force me, despite myself, to wish for celebrity in letters, be assured, *Monsieur*, that I would not begin my literary career by accusing a man of intelligence, whom I have not the privilege of knowing personally and from whom I have received only marks of esteem.

I have the honour of being, *Monsieur*, your very humble and obedient servant,

F. ROBERT, *née* BAZIN.

The following report written by Abbé Sicard appeared in *Le Moniteur*. *Tr*.

REPORT MADE TO *Son Excellence le Ministre de l'Intérieur* ON THE PRETENDED HEALING OF DEAF-MUTES PERFORMED BY M. FABRE D'OLIVET.

January 31st, 1812.

Monseigneur:

On Thursday, November 28th, 1811, there gathered at the *Institution impériale des Sourds-Muets* of Paris, the commission named by Your Excellency with a view to verifying the healing of deafness which M. Fabre d'Olivet pretends to have performed upon the said Veillard, congenital deaf-mute. This young man presented himself accompanied by M. Jeuffroy, his master, *professeur de l'École impériale de gravure sur pierres fines*. Before proceeding to the examination of the actual state of this deaf-mute, the commission perused various papers relative to the affair which had been sent to them by M. le baron Pasquier, *préfet de police.* These papers, three in number, are the report of M. Jeuffroy, the examination of M. Fabre d'Olivet by *M. le préfet de police,* and that to which Mlle. Rathe, instigator of the abduction of Veillard, was likewise subjected.

It results from the reading of these three papers, (*a*) that after several intrigues unknown to M. Jeuffroy, Mlle. Rathe called at the home of this artist, and having obtained from him permission to take Veillard to the country, under pretext of having him model a portrait, had him clandestinely conducted to a boarding-school for young ladies where M. Fabre d'Olivet lives; (*b*) that having arrived at this house, Veillard submitted to a kind of treatment which Mlle. Rathe designates under the name of *opération* and which M. Fabre d'Olivet carefully limits himself to indicating by vague words about the application of a curative principle to the auditive faculty; (*c*) that at the end of a week's sojourn with M. Fabre d'Olivet, Veillard was brought back to M. Jeuffroy who found him as deaf as before, although Mlle. Rathe and M. Fabre d'Olivet declared him on the road to recovery; (*d*) that having obtained from his master, by motives which one can only applaud, permission to return to M. Fabre d'Olivet in order to complete his pretended healing, he went there each morning for a week, which makes in all seventeen days. The achievement of the cure, fixed for that time by M. Fabre d'Olivet, did not correspond to his promises and to the hopes of Veillard.

After the reading of these three papers, the commission heard M. Jeuffroy, who thought he ought to communicate to us certain circumstances he had omitted in his report or learned after he had sent it to M. *le conseiller-d'état, préfet de police.* According to this verbal declaration, Veillard, taken away secretly during the night to M. Fabre d'Olivet, is said to have been introduced into the house by a back doorway; to have remained three days shut up in a room, without communication with anyone; and when his brain had undoubtedly been greatly excited or rather considerably weakened by this kind of initiation to the miracle that was about to be performed on him, to have been made to swear upon the Gospel not to reveal to anyone the secret manœuvres of which he was about to be the witness and the object.

In fact, we have more than one proof of the influence that has been exercised over the mind of this young man, in the report that he himself presented to us upon his pretended healing, and even in the responses he made to the questions we addressed to him in writing.

His report largely confirms all that M. Jeuffroy has written upon the manner in which the carrying off of this young man was conducted, and gives besides to this action, by the admission of a secret correspondence established between Veillard and M. Fabre d'Olivet, a character of premeditation which renders this stratagem still more worthy of reproach. But the most remarkable part of this report, that which shows to what point the mind of this young man was bewitched, is the narration of the progress of his healing. He has heard, he says, the words *papa, mama,* the barking of dogs, the sound of the clock, etc. These facts, the falseness of which will be seen in the result of the tests to which the commission subjected young Veillard, are intermingled with certain almost mystic phrases which, suggesting the style of M. Fabre d'Olivet, make one think that the latter is not stranger to the editing of this report. Such, among others, is this one: *I want to tell you that my sense of hearing resembles a thick fog which prevents discerning and distinguishing objects; it is necessary to await the coming of the sun to dissipate it.* In a letter of M. Fabre d'Olivet, in response to one the commission wrote to invite him to appear before it, one remarks these words: "The deaf-mute given over to the examination of the commission should, when the principle is developed in him by the appropriate cultivation, be able to hear, understand and comprehend as a man endowed at birth with the auditive faculty, in the same manner as a seed planted in the ground ferments there, develops, and produces with the time and cultivation necessary, a perfect plant according to its kind."

It seems to us that the phrase of Veillard is nothing but a part detached from that of M. Fabre d'Olivet, and that *the sun which dissipates the fog to give hearing* is indeed the same which makes *the auditive faculty ferment, develop and produce, as a seed deposited in the ground.*

In the examination the commission made Veillard undergo, it was particularly interested in drawing from him a disclosure of the means used to effect his pretended healing. But this young man, bound by an oath which he regards as sacred, constantly refused to give any explanation upon this point. In truth there remained very little for the commission to learn from him, for he declares in his report that medicines had been poured into his ears; and whilst seeking to deny what he had at first confessed to M. Jeuffroy, the administering of a purgative beverage, his last response nearly confirmed this admission. In order to obtain this confession, the commission apparently renounced it, and limited itself to finding out in what vessel the purgative had been contained. But he replied that he could not tell because the vessel would disclose the remedy.

Nothing more remained to complete the examination of this affair, except to verify carefully the deafness of Veillard and to be assured whether or not this infirmity was really healed or at least diminished. In order to confirm or invalidate this charge, it was necessary to determine his former condition and to be aided to this end with information which might not be suspected of partiality. We believe one could regard as such that which was furnished us by the master of this young man, M. Jeuffroy, who, living habitually with his pupil for five years, was able to know better than anyone else the degree of Veillard's deafness. This artist assured us positively that, like a great number of deaf-mutes, Veillard had the faculty of perceiving noises and certain sounds more or less loud, such as that from a gun, or from an orchestra. This Veillard could not deny. Proceeding from this report, we were able to compare him with what he was before his sojourn with M. Fabre d'Olivet, and we did not notice that his hearing was sensibly ameliorated.

A member of the commission, standing behind him, began by articulating in an ordinary voice, some very distinct words, particularly those which Veillard pretended to have heard at M. Fabre d'Olivet's, such as *papa, mama,* and his ears were not struck by them. The voice was raised; same result. A bell was used; his attention was prepared by its being shown to him; it was percussed with loud blows behind him and he was asked to count the blows plainly by signs; no evidence of audition. A large table was brought and in order that the percussion should not be communicated to the feet of the deaf-mute by the shaking of the floor, it was held up in the air for isolation. It was struck on the top with a large key, without

Veillard's showing himself sensitive to this new noise. The last blow, however, struck with great force, was really heard. Veillard turned his head quickly and gave proof of audition, but no more or no less than he had given at other times, according to one of his old comrades who was present at the experiment.

Such are the results of the examination to which the commission submitted this young man concerning the sense of hearing. It results from this examination and from all the documents with which we have been furnished, that young Veillard, after having been taken by stratagem to M. Fabre d'Olivet's, underwent there, and without any success, a treatment internal as well as external.

Now what idea can one form of the conduct of M. Fabre d'Olivet? It is repugnant to the commission to regard this individual as an artful charlatan who would apply all the intelligence and learning he may have, to lead the mind of a poor deaf-mute astray and to pass himself off in certain enlightened circles for a great worker of miracles. The commission does not believe it ought to judge him so unfavourably; it thinks that he has deceived others only because he is deceived, and that he

himself is the greatest dupe of his chimerical pretensions and of his inexperience.

To explain this kind of enigma, it is necessary
to recall here certain reflections deduced from the
observation of deaf-mutes and apply them to the
examination of the first cure which M. Fabre
d'Olivet, in his investigation by the police, in
several letters inserted in the daily papers and even
in a pamphlet which he has published on this
subject, is said to have made upon Rodolphe
Grivel, congenital deaf-mute. To prove that this
healing is false and illusory is to overthrow the
pretensions raised upon that of Veillard and to
enlighten what is still obscure and mysterious in
this affair.

All deaf-mutes are not wholly deprived of hearing. A great number of them are born with a
certain degree of audition which, being insufficient
to adapt itself to the ordinary functions of the
organ, is weakened more and more through in-
action, without, however, being completely destroyed. If the ears of these are submitted to
gradual exercises, not only is the slight sensibility
with which they were at first endowed recalled,
but it is augmented at least to the point of convert-

ing the congenital deafness into a simple hardness
of hearing. This view is not a simple hypo-
thesis. Five years ago, one of the members of
the commission presented to *la Société de l'École
de Médecine*, six deaf-mutes whom he had brought
by this very means to the state of a child *hearing
and speaking*.

Chance placed in the hands of M. Fabre d'Olivet
the deaf-mute who was unquestionably the most
fitted for this sort of physiological education. This
young man, who lived several years at the *Sourds-
Muets de Paris*, was known there as being gifted
with much intelligence and with a great facility
for hearing and speaking. These two faculties
had appeared so little weakened to the physician
of the institution that he had written several times
to the parents, offering them, if they would facilitate the means for him, to reëstablish completely
the hearing and speech of this child. A reply
from his mother which has been preserved, admits
the incomplete deafness of her son, and relates the
cause of this infirmity to a running of the ear
which began in infancy. His mother complained
to several persons whose testimony could if necessary be called upon, that her son, whom M. l'abbé

Sicard showed in entertainments as speaking, had
lost rather than gained in the institution as far
as speech was concerned. In fact he said only
a few words, but more than sufficient to give proof
of audition. All the employés in the house were
witnesses. It was also remarked that, by an
imitation purely spontaneous, he caught the cries
of certain animals, etc. Such is the young man
whom M. Fabre d'Olivet asserts to have healed
of congenital deafness. The least disadvantageous
thought one can entertain of the pretended healing
is, that after having applied his remedy, or to
express it better and to enter into his ideas, after
having breathed in his *auditive principle*, he wished
to know the results of this kind of *incubation*, and,
struck with astonishment to see Grivel give signs
of audition, he wished to believe and to cry out,
miracle! The same error would no doubt have
deceived him on the subject of Veillard. His ears,
subjected during several days to the action of
violent sounds, would be reanimated and perhaps
show themselves sensitive to certain noises until
then unperceived.

In whatever indulgent manner one may consider the chimerical cures performed by M. Fabre

d'Olivet, one may leave him to delight in the illusions of his brilliant discoveries; but it would be dangerous not to unveil the secret and the proof of his errors. Above all it is important, in respect for the laws with which he is in contravention, that it be no longer permitted for a man who is neither physician nor surgeon to take possession blindly of one of the most obscure parts of the art of healing; and whereas the government prescribes that all secret remedies be disclosed by all possessors of those occult means, M. Fabre d'Olivet alone continues to give importance to his, enveloping them with the veil of mystery and hiding them, in some way, in the obscurity of the Kabbalistic science.

Signed: Portal; Percy; l'abbé Sicard, *membre de l'Institut;* Itard, *médecin de l'Institution des Sourds-Muets de Paris.*

EXTRACTS FROM SEVERAL LETTERS WRITTEN TO THE
EDITOR OF *Le Journal de Lyon.*

Copied by the Translator from a pamphlet belonging
to the Bibiliothèque Nationale.

The new phenomena which have taken place
quite recently at Aubenas and at Lyon, in the
development of hearing among many congenital
deaf-mutes, having seemed to us of particular interest, as much for the good of humanity as for
the advancement of the sciences in general, we
have believed it advisable to bring together the
several letters which have been written upon this
subject to the Editor of *le Journal,* so as to form
a sort of supplement to "La Guérison de Rodolphe Grivel"* published at Montpellier by
M. Fabre d'Olivet. We hope that the reader will
be kindly disposed toward us for this labour, by
appreciating the pure and disinterested intention
that has made us undertake it.

* Brochure in 8°, chez Sivalle, libraire, Grande Rue à Montpellier;
à Lyon chez Maire, libraire, rue Mercière; et à Paris, chez Treuttel et
Wurtz. (1819.)

LETTER FROM MONSIEUR EMBRY, D.M.M.

Membre du Juri médical du département de l'Ardèche, médecin-inspecteur des Eaux minérals de Vals.

AUBENAS, (Ardèche), April 6th, 1819.

Monsieur,

I have read in *le Journal du Commerce*, of March 22nd, the announcement of two phenomena effected at Privas by M. Fabre d'Olivet, upon two young girls, congenital deaf-mutes, to whom this savant gave hearing by means known only to himself. I have not had the pleasure of seeing these two young girls; but the reality of the phenomena is beyond doubt by the testimony of persons of a merit and a probity far from all suspicion. Also it can be verified since these two girls are living, the one in Privas and the other in Pouzin. As for myself, who have studied and practised medicine for more than thirty years, I must in truth say that I have found nothing either in theory, or in practice which approaches what has been told me and what I have seen; also I cannot refrain from feeling that the account of the correspondent and the remarks of the *journaliste du Commerce* are insufficient and very cold in a matter of such importance. In order not to call censure upon myself, I am giving some circumstantiated details upon what I have seen and heard.

One of the foremost inhabitants of this town, knowing of the events at Privas, presented his son, a deaf-mute, to M. Fabre d'Olivet, who promised to make some sojourn in Aubenas as he returned to Paris from the interior of the Cevennes. While he was occupied with this child, a woman from Villeneuve-de-Berg, named Anne Barbe, more than forty-nine years old, well known in the whole town as being a congenital deaf-mute, never having given any sign of audition or uttered any articulate word, came and threw herself at his feet. M. Fabre d'Olivet refused at first, undoubtedly because of the advanced age of his subject; but finally, moved by her tears, and urged by all the members of her respected family, he consented to risk the issue. I scarcely dare to tell you, *Monsieur*, what the success of it was. This woman, having arrived on the 31st of March, heard all noises the Wednesday following. Thursday morning I myself saw her count, by raising a finger, the taps struck upon a small drum; distinguish and designate whether the wood of the case or the skin had been struck; give attention to the sound of a violin, following its cadence; grasp the inflection of the voice, and articulate distinctly several words, such as *pain, vin, eau, pot, bas, papa, tata,* etc. She departed the same day for Villeneuve, where she continues her progress.

I have believed, *Monsieur,* that you might think as I, that these details are worthy of attention; when one has been a witness it is impossible to resist the desire of publishing them. I pass in silence, reluctantly, over details concerning the signs of audition in two children of four or five years of age to whom M. Fabre d'Olivet has been willing to give his attentions. The number of individuals, deaf-mute or affected with accidental deafness more or less complete, is considerable. Every day they present themselves; one man alone could not suffice to treat them all. The discovery of M. Fabre d'Olivet seems to me of high importance, and, as much as I can judge, will not be limited to the treatment of the ear alone. Men of the art might be able to extend the application, when they shall have the knowledge of a means sufficiently energetic to render life to an organ apparently bereft of it, and at the same time so painless that little children submit to it without resistance. My only purpose in stating the new successes of M. Fabre d'Olivet is to call to them the attention of a paternal government, which should hasten to give to unfortunates the means to recover a sense the privation of which impairs existence. However, I do not know what the views of M. Fabre d'Olivet are. As to the indirect criticism of the *journaliste du Commerce*, that M. Fabre d'Olivet envelops himself with secrets and mysteries, I do not think it is well-founded. Every man is master of his property; knowledge also is a property. Our charter assures for each one the enjoyment of his goods; and authors, journalists and those who follow the liberal arts, do not give their talents for nothing.

LETTERS FROM M. BOURRIT

Pasteur-Président du Consistoire de Lyon.

Monsieur,

The letter of M. *le docteur* Embry, inserted in your *Journal* of the 16th inst., and the article of *le Journal du Commerce* of March 22nd, relative to the healing of deaf-mutes by M. Fabre d'Olivet at Privas, Aubenas and Aigues-vives, have determined me to make known to the public certain details which are not devoid of interest.

In Geneva I knew, in his infancy, young Rodolphe Grivel of Aubonne, Switzerland, a congenital deaf-mute. I knew at the time of the inutility of all the attempts made by several physicians to give him the faculty of hearing, and of the resolution taken by his estimable mother to conduct him to Paris to abbé Sicard. This young man was there for several years, and appeared many times in public exercises of the establishment, which circumstance alone would suffice to confirm that he was completely deaf and dumb. Called to Paris on business, I had the good fortune there of becoming acquainted with M. Fabre d'Olivet, of forming a friendship with him, and being witness to the healing that he effected upon young Grivel.

It seemed as though the circumstances accompanying such a prodigy must excite the keenest interest in favour of M. Fabre d'Olivet, but on the contrary, his discovery met almost nothing but jealousy, contradiction and unbelief; malice even armed the authorities against him; and far from being encouraged in his precious discovery, in order to keep his peace of mind he was obliged to guard his secret, and thenceforth to occupy himself only with the literary and scientific researches which have assured him a distinguished rank among orientalists and savants.

Nevertheless young Grivel, having received hearing, and having no further need of help from signs, returned to Switzerland where he not only conserved the faculty of hearing but also perfected himself greatly in that of speaking. My wife, my children and myself can certify to having seen him each year participating in social games in which it is necessary to hear and speak; we have conversed many times with him and acquired the full conviction of the efficacy of the processes of M. Fabre; but, as it is the truth and nothing more that I wish to present, I must confess that the voice of M. Grivel is not pleasant, that it is somewhat husky and harsh, if I dare express myself thus; but he hears and speaks, that is the essential fact.* He is persevering, and undoubtedly if this young man had been placed under the care of M. Fabre in his infancy, at that age when the

* M. Bourrit has seen M. Grivel since the first appearance of this letter and he confirms all its contents.

organ of speech adapts itself easily to the imitation of all kinds of sounds and noises, there would have been little difference between his manner of speaking and that of persons born with all the senses.

A second occurrence to which I was a witness, in Ganges six months ago, was the restoration of hearing to the mother of a family, deaf for many years; it had been twelve days since M. Fabre had undertaken her cure, and already, at a distance of four feet, she could sustain conversation without fatigue.

Besides the cures performed by M. Fabre in Privas upon the children of M. *le pasteur* Tromparen and at Aigues-vives upon those of M. *le pasteur* Maraval, I learned from M. Fabre through a letter from Privas dated the 22nd of April last, that he there had had the good fortune to develop, in less than ten days, the auditive faculty of six deaf-mutes of various ages and of both sexes, the healing of whom presented very remarkable phenomena.

M. Fabre will arrive soon in Lyon where he will undoubtedly be no less fortunate than elsewhere.

Le Journal du Commerce, without questioning the reality of the cures accomplished by M. Fabre, accuses him of enveloping his discovery *in secrets and mysteries, as would a mystagogue or thaumaturgist of Memphis or of Eleusis,* and this, because he *vigorously rubbed the ears* of one of his patients. It seems to me that there is nothing in that for which M. Fabre should be ridiculed. If he disguises his processes, he has the right to do so; his discovery is his property, and it is right that he take certain precautions in order that its advantages be preserved. I have reason to believe that he would be imprudent at least, if he made public a secret of which charlatanism and ignorance might make evil use; furthermore, he has a soul too noble to wish to carry to the tomb a discovery so interesting as his. What matter, indeed, certain forms that seem somewhat strange, and even, if one wish, mysterious, since they accompany veritable benefits?

Persons who desire to understand more fully that which concerns the development of the sense of hearing as procured for the deaf by M. Fabre, should read the work he has just published in Montpellier on the subject. This work, entitled *Notions sur le Sens de l'Ouïe,* will not, in some respects, please everyone, and above all the author of the article inserted in *le Journal du Commerce;* but it contains too many things worthy of attention not to be read with the liveliest interest.

Monsieur,

In my letter of April 30th last, upon the healing of deaf-mutes by M. Fabre d'Olivet, I referred the readers to his *Notions sur le Sens de l'Ouïe;* but, although in its second edition, this work is not yet in the bookshop of Lyon. Moreover, the arrival of my friend, and the cures he has already made, especially that of Madame Caroline Duclos, a deaf-mute twenty-three years old, which succeeded perfectly, have occasioned so many comments, and provoked so many questions, that I believe it useful, not to make a complete analysis of the work, but to give extracts and bring together the things that appear to me fitting to rectify the false ideas many people give themselves concerning the immediate effect of the means * which gives

* M. Fabre d'Olivet calls *means* that which, known in the ancient sanctuaries and quite clearly expressed in the first chapters of the Sepher, can facilitate the transference of life into an organ which is deprived of it.

to the deaf the auditive faculty. It is deplorable
that someone, more versed than I am in a subject
of this nature, has not undertaken this task. The
public and I myself would have gained thereby;
but the hope of being useful outweighs my pride,
and I appeal to the indulgence of the readers for
this letter and those following, in view of the
motive that has caused me to take up the pen.

The Preliminary Explanations of the work, *Notions sur le Sens de l'Ouïe*, are, in part, consecrated
to clearing M. Fabre d'Olivet from the blame of
having been able, since 1811, epoch of the healing
of M. Grivel, until last autumn, to pass so many
years without letting those persons afflicted with
deafness enjoy his precious discovery. Whence
has come the false inference that either he was
an·unpardonable egotist or did not possess the
means of healing he claimed?

Although this part of the work does not treat
of the fundamental character of *Notions*, etc., it is
however extremely interesting for the piquant narration of the various labours of the author; of
the obstacles the malevolence of Napoleon constantly raised against all his undertakings; of the
persecutions of which he was the object; and of

the motives, unfortunately too legitimate, that reduced him to the impossibility of utilizing his admirable means. It will also be seen in these Preliminaries, and no doubt with much surprise, how M. Fabre d'Olivet, who is not a medical man, owes his great discovery to his researches in the Cosmogony of the Hebrews. In this extraordinary, I might almost say gigantic work upon Genesis which he has undertaken and published under the title of "La Langue Hébraïque Restituée," * he claims that, without annihilating the vulgar tradition of the Sepher of Moses, he has recovered the hieroglyphic meaning, lost for twenty-four centuries. He supports his translation (accompanied by a new grammar and a new radical vocabulary) with all the proofs that comparison with the Samaritan and Chaldaic, the Syriac and Arabic idioms could afford.

Although I may be far from being convinced of the solidity of such a system, I acknowledge that to attack it a similar mass of learning is necessary. It is easier to criticize it than to prove its falsity. In order to combat M. Fabre d'Olivet with equal weapons, it would be necessary to possess, as he

---

* This book is to be had *chez* Maire, *libraire*, at Lyon.

does, nearly all known tongues, to have compared
them one with another and add thereto, in as high
degree, the almost universality of human learning.
What I am saying is in no wise to flatter him, my
opinion is of too little value; it is to warn anyone
disposed to appeal to my friend for relief from
deafness and dumbness that he is not one of those
vulgar men who have only audacity, one of those
quacks whom it is necessary to challenge, but a
distinguished savant whose intentions are pure, and
whose principal desire is to be useful to humanity.

I have said that it was important to meet the
false ideas that too many people have concerning
the immediate effect of the means employed to
restore the auditive faculty to deaf-mutes. Most
of the persons who see a deaf-mute to whom M.
Fabre d'Olivet restores hearing, imagine that he
ought to pass immediately to the condition of
those who have always possessed it. Led astray
by the double meaning attached to the word
entendre, they do not consider the fact that hearing
sounds is neither to seize them nor to classify
them, still less to give them a signification.

Now the deaf-mute must pass through all the
phases of *audition*, of *distinction* and of *classifica-*

tion, in order to arrive at *comprehension*. Is it therefore astonishing that a deaf-mute who has just received a faculty of which it was formerly impossible for him to form the least idea, and who experiences for the first time the impression of noise and of sound, finds himself as a new being placed in a new sphere?

The process which recalls to life the auditive organ previously paralysed, cannot give him at the same instant that force and that consistency which are the result of habit and of time. The ear must still be, for a long time, a delicate instrument which requires watchful care; the brain, disturbed by the new effect of sonorous vibrations, experiences a fatigue that it dreads; and the mind, being able at first to perceive only noises without signification, far from finding any charm in them, often even without suspecting future advantages, suffers and becomes sad. This moment, so beautiful, which restores to man his greatest means for intellectual and moral perfectionism, far from occasioning in him the transports of joy, of wonder and of gratitude for which the witnesses wait, often presents only the sad spectacle of a being as stupid as though fallen from the moon, and sometimes even recalcitrant. Does he suspect his good fortune? He has only acquired the instrument, without a presentiment of its advantages. It is by the care of his relatives and friends, by instruction, by time, that he can learn how to make use of it.

Monsieur,

I must, in accordance with my promise, continue the analysis of the work of M. Fabre d'Olivet upon the sense of hearing; but the progress of events is so precipitate that, despite all the interest in a new theory developed with great talent and made easy to grasp by remarkable clarity of style, I run the risk of causing impatience in your readers, all of whom, more or less acquainted with the healings wrought by M. Fabre d'Olivet, are eager to know the details.

Moreover, those who would investigate this matter and understand the principles of the author, will hasten to obtain his book; and those who, without being interested in science, have a heart rejoicing in everything that can diminish human infirmities, will be glad I have abandoned the theory, in order to state the facts which augur

Appendix

for so many unfortunates the restoration of a sense without which man necessarily remains below himself, loses the major part of the delights of social life, and, as in the midst of emptiness, dwells sadly in a silent world.

Only fifteen days ago M. Fabre d'Olivet came to Lyon and already two children of M. Chatelet, a merchant, the thirteen year old son of M. Parrel, a dyer, the Demoiselles Suc and Paillod, also thirteen, and Madame Caroline Duclos, aged twenty-three years, *enceinte* for the second time, have recovered their hearing, are beginning to distinguish various sounds, are repeating words, even sentences, and attaching to them the meaning they express. The first two, not old enough to fix their attention, do not yet speak, but they understand; and no doubt time will set the seal upon the happiness of their estimable father. All these cases of native deafness have yielded in a few hours to the powerful efficacy of the means of M. Fabre d'Olivet, and this without surgical operation, without internal remedies, without application, without precautionary measures and without uncomfortable consequences.

But, you will say, where, before whom and how

were these astonishing healings done? At the house of M. Mottet, *président de la Chambre de Commerce*, one of the men of our city justly entitled to esteem and general consideration; in the presence of most conspicuous persons, of several public functionaries: M. le baron Rambaud, *maire* of Lyon; le Marquis Dolomieu; M. Panis from Marseilles and several medical men, among others MM. Parat and Desgranges. No one was denied admittance. The experiments were made without preparation, with the most gracious simplicity; they were reiterated almost every day and finally repeated at the home of M. de Permon, *lieutenant-général de police*. It is at the invitation of this respected magistrate, and of M. Mottet, much more than for my friend, that I am writing of these experiments so interesting for humanity.

All the deaf-mutes I have named were placed turn by turn upon a chair in the midst of a numerous assembly and were submitted to (*a*) the test of the drum, which was beaten quite near them, at first behind their heads, then at a greater distance and finally outside the room. Without exception, all counted upon their fingers or even named distinctly the number of blows struck, and indicated whether the blow had been struck upon the skin of the instrument or upon the drum case; (*b*) the test of the flageolet and violin which was first made with the simple scales ascending and descending, the subjects expressing with the head whether they heard or not. Here was observed what M. Fabre d'Olivet has recorded in his *Notions sur le Sens de l'Ouïe*, that the ear perceives the tones from low to high, that the lowest notes are heard first, and that the ascending scale is extended from one day to another according to the development of the ear.

There have been, however, some rather singular deviations from the rule: for example, young Parrel was for several days stationary upon *mi*, without hearing *fa*, although it was only a question of a demi-tone; at last *fa* penetrated, but at first only in part, and *sol* has not yet been heard, whereas *la*, although higher, entered almost without difficulty; a remarkable phenomenon, but justified beforehand by the theory in the book *Notions*, etc.

The test of the violin was pushed further, to find out if, by indiscriminate playing, sometimes on one string, sometimes on another, the subjects could grasp the difference so as to indicate the string played upon. Madame Duclos was rarely mistaken. When modulations of the flageolet or the violin were played behind her, she raised or lowered her hands with admirable correctness, and by a kind of undulating, graceful movement, always in accord with the animated expression of her physiognomy, proved that she heard perfectly the slightest sounds, and with infinite pleasure. M. Fabre d'Olivet has remarked that she has the musical sign designated by doctor Gall. Now, how is it that such a tendency is found when an organ has been paralysed from birth, and that after twenty-three years of deafness it showed itself so sensitive to melody? The demoiselle Peillod also seemed to like music very much. The subjects have distinguished the noise of glass; and when a shield was dropped behind them, at the noise of its fall, they turned around quickly to raise it. They have likewise heard the ticking of a watch and the strike of a repeater.

But the most interesting proofs, unquestionably, are those which have produced speech. Here I pray the reader to recall what I have already said concerning the numberless difficulties to be overcome in order that the sensation of noises and

sounds be transformed into sentiment, and that
the understanding effect discontinuance of the
muteness of the vocal organ, so as to repeat the
inflections of the voice, to form syllables and
group them into words.

The restoration of hearing seems impossible, but
this kind of miracle is the work of a few hours for
M. Fabre d'Olivet; however the obstacles which
remain to be surmounted so that the individual
to whom he restores hearing may use it as we do,
are immense; according to the degree of attention
and the natural disposition of the subjects, their
vocal education will require one, two or even several
years. These considerations are necessary in order
to feel the keen interest inspired by the experiments of which I have spoken, and the results of
which give for the future such beautiful hopes.

Monosyllables well articulated in a full voice
have been pronounced close to the ear of these
former deaf-mutes; all have repeated them and
almost without difficulty. From monosyllables
they have passed to words: there has been hesitation over certain initial letters easily confused
with others: but several repetitions have sufficed
to make the difference distinguished. Afterward,

with the words known and repeated, short sentences have been composed, such as the following addressed to Madame Duclos: "Do you know the mayor of Lyon?" She replied, "No, Monsieur. He is called Rambeau." This magistrate had been pointed out to her; and, as she knows how to read, writing was used so that the sounds might awaken the ideas, and memory hold them together. Following this method, the name of M. Rambeau was inserted in various questions which she comprehended and to which she responded. It is impossible for those who have not been witnesses to imagine to what point the interest in these diverse lessons was aroused; each difficulty surmounted became a sort of triumph in which everyone participated. Finally, when Madame d'Antoine invited Madame Duclos to say after her: "I am very thankful, Monsieur, for what you have done for me; I like M. Fabre d'Olivet," this young woman, moved by the energetic feeling of gratitude, made a great effort and, notwithstanding the length of the sentence, she repeated it with such a true accent, accompanied by an expression so touching, that while I forced myself to refrain from tears, I saw the assemblage impelled by the same excitement to weep with emotion and with joy.

Indeed, what moment is there like that in which parents for the first time hear their child repeat "I love papa!" "I love mama!" What perspective for the deaf-mute who feels himself a new being! And you Fabre d'Olivet, my friend, what have you experienced? I know; the joy of an honest man! Your modest calm shows that it is less the love for glory than that for humanity which vivifies your talents. Ah, my friend! pursue, pursue the noble career Providence has opened for you; be not disturbed by calumniators, by the jealous, by the ingrates who are bent upon injuring you; and the force of truth will give to you the justice that is your due.

The means being found of rendering hearing to the deaf, the only thing lacking is teachers to cultivate audition and apply it to speech. Mesdames Royer and d'Antoine, who have displayed great zeal in behalf of the deaf-mutes healed by M. Fabre d'Olivet, will complete his work; and doubtless a paternal government will take the measures in its power to allow all France to enjoy a discovery so admirable and so worthy to claim its beneficent attention.